"My name is Alan Brauer. I'm a psychiatrist—a medical doctor who helps people learn to change their behavior. My wife, Donna, assists me as a counselor and therapist. Together we train couples in ESO: Extended Sexual Orgasm—the art of making climax last much longer than anyone ever thought possible.

"ESO is not merely extended foreplay. Nor is it some ancient system of subtle spiritual disciplines. It is more than multiple orgasm. It is deep, continuous female orgasm lasting thirty minutes to an hour or more. It is male first-stage orgasm lasting equally as long.

"See for yourself by learning ESO yourself. With training and a willing partner, you can make the most intense physical pleasure that human beings ever feel go on as long as you want it to. This book tells how."

ESO*

How You and Your Lover Can Give Each Other Hours of

*Extended Sexual Orgasm

Alan P. Brauer, M.D., and Donna Brauer

WARNER BOOKS

A Time Warner Company

This book is dedicated to the pioneer sex researchers whose work has influenced our present investigations, and to our clients, whose willing participation has validated our teaching methods.

Edited by Richard Rhodes

Copyright © 1983 by Alan P. Brauer
All rights reserved.
Warner Books, Inc., 1271 Avenue of the Americas, New York, NY 10020

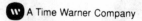 A Time Warner Company

Printed in the United States of America
First trade paperback printing: February 1984
20 19 18 17

Library of Congress Cataloging in Publication Data

Brauer, Alan P.
  ESO™: how you and your lover can give each other hours of extended sexual orgasm.

  Bibliography: p. 215
  Includes index.
  1. Sex instruction.   2. Orgasm.   I. Brauer, Donna.
II. Title.   III. Title: ESO.™
HQ31.B772   1983   613.9′6   82-50863
ISBN 0-446-38645-6 (U.S.A.)

Book design: H. Roberts Design

ABOUT ALAN P. BRAUER, M.D., AND DONNA BRAUER

Dr. Alan Brauer is a psychiatrist, a graduate of the University of Rochester, Rochester, New York, and the University of Michigan School of Medicine. He interned at New York University's Bellevue Hospital in New York City and completed his psychiatric residency at Stanford University in California in 1976. The founder and first director of the Stanford Medical Center Biofeedback and Stress Reduction Clinic, he now serves as clinical assistant professor in the Stanford Department of Psychiatry and Behavioral Sciences. Dr. Brauer is a diplomate of the American Board of Psychiatry and Neurology. He founded and directs the Brauer Stress and Pain Control Medical Center in Palo Alto, California. His work has been published in scientific journals and he has appeared on television and radio throughout the United States.

Donna Brauer, a trained psychotherapist, is his cotherapist and his wife. They have two children. Together, the Brauers have worked extensively in the treatment of sexual problems and in developing and teaching methods of enhancing sexual pleasure, as well as in a broad-based practice of behavioral medicine.

CONTENTS

ILLUSTRATIONS

1

THE PROMISE OF PLEASURE

MY NAME is Alan Brauer. I'm a psychiatrist—a medical doctor who helps people learn to change their behavior. My wife, Donna, assists me as a counselor and therapist. We have a thriving, challenging center in Palo Alto, California.

In 1975 we heard from a married couple doing sex research that they had discovered how to make climax—sexual orgasm—last much longer than anyone has ever thought possible. Not seconds longer or minutes longer. *Hours* longer, they said. They also said it was wonderful.

We were skeptical. Sex therapy is an important part of our practice. We've treated many clients with sexual problems and we've studied the scientific literature. Dr. William Masters and Virginia Johnson, the pioneer sex researchers, clocked female orgasm in their experimental subjects at an average four to twelve seconds per climax. Dr. Seymour Fisher, in his thorough 1973 study *The Female Orgasm*, discovered a similar average—six to ten seconds. Masters and Johnson and Fisher have noted that a few exceptional women experience unusually intense orgasms that last longer than twenty seconds. Male orgasm has been reported to average about the same few seconds as female.

On the other hand, we have occasionally encountered clients in our practice who describe experiencing unusually long, continuous orgasms lasting from five to fifteen minutes.

The husband and wife who told us about their breakthrough were willing to allow us to observe them making love, which we did, in a structured teaching situation. We saw all the signs of orgasmic response, extended on that particular occasion for almost an hour. Afterward we listened to the couple's explanation of how they learned by trial and error to extend their orgasms. We went home and practiced. Over the next several months we taught ourselves.

We were convinced then from personal experience that vastly extended climax is possible and can be learned. We set out to develop ways to teach others to extend orgasm in a step-by-step, safely structured system in a therapeutic program.

By 1982 we had trained some sixty couples and forty individuals in what we now call ESO™: Extended Sexual Orgasm.*

Besides training couples and individuals during the last several years, we have presented many intensive weekend seminars to medical and health professionals throughout the United States, reporting ESO techniques. A highlight of those seminars is a videotape of a husband sustaining his wife through thirty minutes of extended orgasm.

Approximately fifteen percent of the men and women who attend our weekend seminars report in one-month-follow-up questionnaires that they have achieved some level of ESO.

The couples who are learning ESO are average men and

*Pronounced Eee-Ess-Oh, like ESP or IBM.

women. Some are younger, some older. Some come to us originally with sexual problems. Others are comfortable sexually but want to increase the pleasure they share. More than thirty percent are able to learn ESO within a period of two or three months.

ESO is not merely extended foreplay. It is not simply "multiple orgasm." Nor is it some ancient system of subtle spiritual discipline. *At its ultimate level, for women, ESO is deep, continuous orgasm of ever-increasing arousal lasting thirty minutes to an hour or more.* There are intense, measurable, continuous muscular contractions of two types—superficial and deep. *For men, ESO at its ultimate level is first-stage orgasm, that momentary peak of intense pleasure just before a man feels he is going to ejaculate, extended in time for thirty minutes to an hour or more.* There is hard erection and copious secretion of clear fluid.

ESO embodies a range of experiences at different levels of intensity. For women ESO usually begins with clenching vaginal contractions like those of ordinary, brief orgasm but continuing without any pause or rest between contractions for one minute or more. Each contraction is short, lasting about one second.

At higher levels, female ESO is characterized by longer, push-out contractions of the deep pelvic muscles. Each contraction can last ten seconds or more. It is followed immediately by another push-out contraction or by one or more clenching vaginal contractions lasting several seconds each. We identify this state of mixed deep and shallow contractions as Phase I. It may continue for fifteen minutes or longer. Women experience it subjectively as continuous orgasmic pleasure—rising and leveling but never dropping away. Women in this phase of ESO are aware that they must deliberately reach for sensation to climb higher and avoid dropping away.

At the highest level of female ESO, which we call Phase II, continuous slow waves of push-out contractions of the deep pelvic muscles replace the mixed contractions of Phase I. Each contraction lasts up to thirty seconds and there are no rest periods between. Women experience this phase subjectively as a continuous orgasmic increase. They feel as if they are on a smoothly ascending orgasmic track. They feel as if they don't have to work to stay there. They can drop their level of arousal and stop their ESO experience whenever they or their partners decide. They can very quickly reenter ESO within the next twenty-four hours or so, whenever they and their partners choose. This quick reentry into ESO we call the Rapid Orgasmic Response.

ESO is a range of experiences for men as well. Male orgasm ordinarily consists of two phases: an emission phase lasting three to five seconds, followed by a sense of ejaculatory urgency and then an ejaculation phase of approximately ten contractions lasting about ten seconds. In Phase I ESO the emission phase is extended—to one minute, to ten minutes or more—followed by an intense but not necessarily extended ejaculation phase. Men experience this phase subjectively as sustained orgasmic pleasure. They are aware that they must deliberately concentrate on control techniques to avoid cresting over into ejaculation. That feels like climbing to increased arousal, leveling, climbing higher and leveling again.

At the highest level of male ESO, Phase II, a man finds himself in a continuous state of orgasmic emission for thirty minutes or more. Clear fluid issues almost continuously, drop by drop, from his penis. His anal sphincter is relaxed and open. As with female ESO, he feels as if he is on an orgasmic track, continuously climbing, where he no longer needs to concentrate on holding back his ejaculation. Whenever he or his partner decide, he can ejaculate. The ejaculation phase may involve twenty or more intense contractions and last twenty seconds or more.

If he and his partner wish, a man experienced in Phase II ESO may then, with continued stimulation, maintain full or partial erection and reenter an emission state of orgasm in a very short time after ejaculating—within minutes, even within seconds.

Until the early 1960s—not that long ago, compared to the thousands of years of human history—medical science taught, and almost everyone believed, that human beings could not voluntarily control their heartbeat, their blood pressure, the temperature of their hands, their response to pain. We now know that people can be trained very simply to control all those responses and many more. The discovery was a surprise, late in the history of mankind. The training is now called biofeedback and it's used every day. We use it routinely in our medical practice. If we can learn to influence so many different kinds of bodily responses, why not the orgasmic response too?

More recently the literature of sex therapy has made passing reference to something like extended orgasm in women. Dr. Irene Kassorla's book *Nice Girls Do* discusses a "maxi orgasm." Dr. Kassorla describes it as "feeling deeper, more concentrated, more intense—after having two or three dozen orgasms, the vagina seems to take over and the orgasms occur in repeated fashion with only moments of rest in between . . . and orgasming for two hours or more. . . ."

Alice Kahn Ladas, Beverly Whipple, and John D. Perry, in *The G Spot*, which was published while our book was in press, mention some women who have " 'multiple ejaculatory orgasms,' sometimes lasting up to an hour or more. . . ."

There have been isolated reports in scientific journals (Dobbins and Jensen, 1978, for example) of men who have multiple orgasm without ejaculation.

But despite these reports and hints of something more than ordinary, brief orgasm or than multiple orgasm, we know of no book or journal that describes these intensely pleasurable states in detail or explains, step by step, *how to achieve them*. Until now: until *ESO*.

The discovery that both male and female orgasm can be extended for long periods of time was more than a surprise. It was a shock. You may find it hard to believe. Many people do at first. But you don't have to take our word for it. You can see for yourself—by learning ESO yourself. The most intense physical pleasure that human beings ever feel can be extended. With training, you can extend your experience of continuous orgasm to a minute or five minutes or half an hour or more. You need a willing partner, a developing sense of trust, and time.

This book tells how.

II

CREATING THE CONDITIONS FOR PLEASURE

For Couples

We assume at the outset that you are reading this book because you want to increase your sexual pleasure. We will offer a variety of programs and exercises to help you do so. They've been tried by hundreds and sometimes even thousands of other men and women, and they work.

You and your partner may decide to follow the program we describe here to extend your orgasms. We hope you will. It's important to start out with realistic expectations. A realistic first goal for most couples would be to extend your orgasms to double or triple their present length. That may mean twenty seconds instead of ten. It may mean a full minute or even two.

Once you've established that new level of experience, you might reasonably consider a more ambitious program of working toward five to ten minutes of continuous orgasm. From that level you might decide to work toward having ESO for a full half an hour, which is what many couples agree is a delightful and suitable ultimate goal. You may spend several months of pleasurable practice before achieving this level of orgasm.

Experiencing ESO for an hour or more may require more months of practice. Not everyone will be sufficiently persistent to achieve it. In our experience, couples who achieve this level of ESO communicate exceptionally well and have large reserves of trust and love.

If you extend your orgasms from six seconds to even one full minute, you will already have increased your time of maximum pleasure by tenfold. That should be cause for celebration. At that point you can, if you wish, decide together to aim for still longer orgasmic experience. After the first major step, you'll find it easier to go on to experience longer periods of ESO.

Most of the basic skills that prepare you for extended orgasm can be learned by self-stimulation. Some men and women have occasionally experienced a low level of ESO alone. But for higher levels of ESO you will need a partner. You need someone you trust who is willing to give you full attention—and then accept your full attention in return. The essence of ESO is both partners giving full attention to one sexual nervous system at a time. This book is written, then, for couples: man and woman, husband and wife, lovers of the same or opposite sex.* Both partners should read it carefully from beginning to end and then discuss it and arrive at agreement on their goals. They may then go back and begin to follow our directions to achieve whatever level of training they've planned.

Many couples find it useful to go through ESO training for the pleasure of the process and not necessarily to extend their orgasms. Other couples may choose to read the entire book and then practice only part of its program—Chapter III, "Developing Skills," for example, or Chapter IV, "Getting Together"—without working on ESO at all.

We can't stress enough the importance of discussing with

---

*Single men and women can train themselves in ESO skills to share when they find a partner. ESO is entirely possible for same-sex couples, male or female, as well. Wherever we discuss a partner of the opposite gender, same-sex couples should read in the appropriate modifications of direction for their gender.

each other fully beforehand how you feel about deciding to expand your sexual experience. Many men and women believe that they would like to experience greater sexual pleasure. But most of us have fears of doing so and hidden doubts. You and your partner must arrive at clear agreement on the principle of increasing your sexuality together. You must also agree on exactly how you wish to accomplish that increase, and you need to share your doubts and hesitations about doing so.

Sometimes one partner attempts to coerce or intimidate the other into agreement. That won't work. Unless you *both* honestly share an equal interest in sexual enhancement, you are likely to encounter problems in achieving change.

If you don't honestly want to pursue extended orgasm, don't agree with your partner to do so. Without honest agreement you'll end up sabotaging your partner's goal. Then he or she, not understanding the sabotage, will feel guilt and blame.

You might agree instead to any number of pleasurable but less ambitious goals we suggest along the way. For example, you might agree simply to do, at a specific time, one of the many exercises we describe. It could even be one of the communication exercises rather than something more specifically sexual. Or you might agree to work with your partner on improving a sexual problem that either of you perceives you have. Limited agreements like these can lay the groundwork for broader agreements in the future. There's much valuable information in this book that you can incorporate into your current lovemaking without pursuing extended orgasm. You can derive significant sexual benefit without making major changes in your sexual commitment. Remember, all of the programs and exercises we suggest are meant to be *fun*. Don't turn them into work.

Our purpose in presenting new information on extended orgasm is not to create new pressures for sexual performance. Rather, we want to open up pleasurable possibilities for adventurous people. Participation is definitely *voluntary*.

Reasons for ESO

Some people, when they hear of ESO, ask why they should bother. For those who need reasons, there are a number of very good ones.

One is that better sex is better for your health. It's good exercise. It stimulates the central nervous system, releases tension, and relieves stress. It stimulates the hormone system to help both men and women stay healthy and young.

A second reason is that ESO improves your mood. An extended orgasm is a tranquilizer better than Valium and an antidepressant better than amphetamines. When you practice ESO with the regularity we suggest in this book, these physical and emotional improvements continue.

Another reason is that people who experience frequent high-quality sex function more efficiently in their other activities. They have more energy to devote to their work, to their family, and to friends.

Still another reason is that better sex strengthens a relationship. Couples who are happier in bed are more likely to be happy together when they're out of bed. Better sex by itself won't save a failing marriage, but it definitely can help. Sex is an important form of communication, and better communication will improve any relationship.

ESO helps make a couple's relationship more secure. They learn to depend on the superior sexual experiences and excellent sexual communication they have achieved. When they attain ESO together, they know they are dedicated to pleasing each other and value each other that much more. They're less likely to seek other partners. They don't want to lose what they've gained.

The most obvious reason for learning ESO is that orgasm is pleasurable. Ask any number of people what experience they have that is intrinsically good. The only experience everyone is likely to agree on is sexual orgasm. Sex is more than orgasm, certainly. But the point of sex is pleasure for yourself and the gift of pleasure to your partner. Orgasm is that pleasure focused most intensely.

Yet the average orgasm is only ten seconds long. The average frequency of intercourse is once or twice a week. That's twenty seconds a week, about one and a half minutes a month, about eighteen minutes a year. In fifty years, that's about fifteen hours. For fifteen hours of ecstasy we devote how many thousands and thousands of hours to thinking about sex, worrying about sex, daydreaming about sex, wishing for sex, planning for sex?

With ESO you can spend more of those hours actually *having* sex. Intensely. You have pleasure and the gift of pleasure to win. You have nothing to lose and much to gain. Some men, when they hear of ESO, immediately feel threatened. They think of how much they struggle to retard ejaculation or to maintain an erection, how hard they work to give their partners pleasure. They visualize that process going on for an hour or more and they panic.

It deserves to be said up front: partners *take turns*—equal and equally pleasurable turns—giving each other ESO, and their primary instruments of stimulation are their hands.

Men and women think and communicate differently, which leads to confusion and misinterpretation both ways. ESO makes sex, at least, less confusing, because partners share similar goals in being deliberate about pleasure. A man learns to understand a woman's sexual needs and to satisfy them fully. As a result, his sexual self-confidence skyrockets. Whatever his age, whatever his previous experience, he learns that he can give his partner enormous pleasure whenever she wants. "The feeling of power is unbelievable," one of our clients told us when his wife began having ESO. "I never knew what I was missing!"

Similarly, men begin paying attention to their own pleasure, not only to what they can do for their partner. When Fred, a shy accountant, married to Carol for eight years, learned ESO, he told us, "Sometimes I get an erection just thinking about our lovemaking now."

Men who come to us reporting problems maintaining erection are delighted to discover that they can thoroughly satisfy their partners with ESO *without erection*. Since that's a less demanding situation, and since their partners' passion is highly erotic to them, their erections usually return.

Some women, when they hear of ESO, worry that it will be too strenuous. It would be if the extended state were as athletically extreme as familiar, brief orgasm. We find instead that after a woman moves into the extended state, her blood pressure, heart rate, and respiration rate drop from their initial peaks, even though she continues intensely in orgasm. The body balances and relaxes, much as it does with meditation, although none of these physical measures drops all the way to the resting rate until after ESO ends. Both men and women then feel relaxed and peaceful.

Women who have felt frustration and bitterness in their relationships with their partners become much less angry, and more content and loving, when they regularly experience ESO. They learn that deep sexual pleasure is their birthright and they learn to assert themselves to have it. Barbara, a client who was hostile to her husband and drifting toward divorce until they worked together to learn ESO, described the change to us. "I used to pick on Hal for everything," she said. "Nothing he did anymore was right. Now he's wonderful, he's my wonderful lover—even though I know he's still doing a lot of the same things that used to make me mad."

Some men and women resist learning ESO because they fear their partners will somehow become insatiable, find other partners, have affairs. To the contrary, couples who learn ESO together almost always become closer, more loving, and more secure. They are grateful to each other; they've learned to depend on each other; they're much less inclined to look elsewhere for sexual excitement. They know how difficult it would be to achieve such excellent communication and such intense satisfaction with a stranger.

Men and women who have lived together for years, couples whose lives have become routine, even report falling in love again when they learn ESO. Bonnie, in her seventh year of marriage, told us about the results of one memorable night of ESO: "I was sitting in a sales meeting the next day. I thought back to our lovemaking the night before and suddenly I found myself turning on. I felt so *connected* to Phil. It was wonderful. I was already looking forward to seeing him again, and it was only ten in the morning."

Discovering *by experience* that vastly more pleasure is possible for you than you ever imagined, even in fantasy, can have an enormous impact on your life. The men and women we know who have learned ESO are more confident, more optimistic, and happier than they have ever been.

Reasons to Postpone ESO

There are conditions when some people should postpone learning ESO. Men and women who have serious heart disease, have suffered a recent stroke, have acute injuries or a serious, chronic illness may want to talk to their doctors first. A guideline: anyone who is able to perform moderate physical exercise should be able to practice ESO.

Couples on the verge of breaking up, couples with serious problems, may need counseling first. If working toward ESO makes your relationship worse rather than better, that's a sign that you need outside help.

Individuals with severe sexual problems may want to seek counseling for those problems before learning ESO. (If you're worried that you qualify, see "Sexual Problems," p. 170, for identification of problem areas and guidance on what to do.)

Otherwise, ESO is a delight to young and old.

Creating Trust

The most important single precondition for ESO is trust. You don't even have to love your partner (it helps), but he or she must be someone you trust. Otherwise you won't allow yourself to become a passive receiver of the pleasure your partner is giving you. You won't be willing to let go.

You create trust with good communication, communication without fear. (For detailed suggestions to help you and your partner communicate, see "Communicating," p. 194.) What you trust your partner to do is to care about your well-being and not deliberately to hurt you, physically or emotionally.

Trust is an important asset in any relationship. It should be valued accordingly and taken seriously. Once it's lost, it's hard to regain. If someone lies to you, you don't easily believe him again. If someone ridicules you, you don't easily put yourself again in his hands.

How can you create trust? Make trust a goal and say so: "I want to trust you. I want you to trust me." Start with simple agreements in nonsexual areas. Work into more serious problem areas from there.

One of the couples we see in therapy, for example, came to us unhappy with how far they had grown apart. They were both involved in their work and didn't spend much time together. Bob's personality is severely analytical, Ellen's extremely emotional.* Potentially they complement each other, but at that time they clashed. Lack of trust was basic to their disagreement.

---

*We're not using real names, and we've changed some details to protect our clients' privacy. That will be true throughout this book. Remember also that most of the men and women we see come to us initially with problems. Even people with problems are able to achieve ESO. Their stories are valuable for identifying and dramatizing ways to improve sexual functioning. Take from them what is useful to you.

Ellen, for example, never knew when Bob would be home for dinner. It infuriated her. She fixed dinner, Bob was late, and dinner was ruined. Bob didn't call to let Ellen know when he would be late, it turned out, because in the past, when he had called, she had argued with him and pressured him to match his work schedule to her dinner plans.

We asked Bob and Ellen to make an agreement: he would call her when he expected to be late; she wouldn't pressure him when he called. A small detail, but a way of building trust. They've kept the agreement and, in this area at least, both of them trust each other more. As a result, they have begun to talk about other areas of conflict. Ellen is moderating her emotionalism. Bob is warming up and talking more about his feelings. They'll need to make other agreements. Equally important, they'll need to keep them. That's how learning to trust each other works.

The Question of Time

Look at the following list of ways people spend time. As you scan it jot down how many minutes or hours you give each week to each activity:

Working	Talking to your sexual partner
Eating	Shopping
Sleeping	Talking on the telephone
Taking care of children	Visiting friends
Watching television	Going to movies/concerts/plays
Cleaning house	Reading books
Playing a sport	Listening to music
Practicing a hobby	Making love

You may be surprised to see how little time you spend in sexual intimacy compared to other activities. You're an exceptional lover if you devote as much as two hours a week to making love. Most people give far more time to watching television (the national average is more than six hours a day per person) than they do to lovemaking. They leave sex unscheduled and catch it when they can.

They do so partly because they believe sex should be "spontaneous." If it's deliberate, they think, then it must be forced. If it's forced, then it must be a burden and a duty rather than an expression of love.

No one learns to dance, swim, or ski "spontaneously," nor does anyone maintain those skills without scheduling time to perform them. Why should an equally subtle, complex skill like sexual pleasuring be different? And why shouldn't deliberately allowing time for intimacy with your partner be counted as an expression of love? It was when you were dating.

In fact, better lovemaking is possible only by giving sex priority in your life. Look again at the weekly activity list. We all have to work, eat, sleep, take care of ourselves and our children. But after those necessities, which activity feels best? Which makes you happiest and makes your partner happiest? Wouldn't you rather enjoy good lovemaking than watch TV?

Scheduling ESO

For ESO, moderate blocks of time must be set aside every week, especially while you are learning. You'll need a major period of time during the weekend, a minimum of an hour and a half, and two shorter periods during the week of at least thirty minutes each. All these times are minimums. If you can find more time, you should. Every day isn't too often.

The idea of giving sex priority and scheduling it is new enough to most people and scary enough to most people that they resist doing so. We'll talk about resistance in more detail later. Right now we only want to mention that failing to find time for ESO is the most universal resistance we've encountered. We often have to ask couples to bring their desk calendars or appointment books into our office so they can agree then and there on times for ESO training and write those times into their schedules. If you and your partner can't arrange a schedule verbally, get out your books and appoint times to be together and write them down.

You'll find that some times are better for you than others, of course. Setting aside several hours on a weekend isn't usually a problem. Locating time on weekdays can be. Couples we work with usually schedule evening times during the week. Those times should not be the half hours just before sleep, because most people are too sleepy then to give pleasuring their full attention. Leave yourself time *after* intimacy to do the things you do to get ready to sleep. If you regularly begin sleep at 10 P.M., schedule your ESO practice time to end at 9:30.

You will probably have to limit or even give up some of your other activities to learn ESO. You'd do that to learn any new skill. Except for the time involved, ESO is free. You need invest only moderate time and a dash of courage. It's worth the time, we promise you!

Maintaining ESO Skills

Week by week as you learn ESO you will experience increasing pleasure in sexual intimacy. The gain is immediate and increasing. Within several months, depending on where you start from, you should find yourself skilled at creating and maintaining orgasm longer than you do now. ESO is open-ended. You can keep on refining your skills.

We've seen no limit to the levels of pleasure possible with continued experience. But ESO can be maintained as a skill, once learned, with sessions of an hour or two once a week. Weekly sessions are necessary to keep muscular and reflex-control skills tuned. They probably also maintain hormone production at suitably high levels.

With such weekly renewal it's also possible to have good *brief* sex at other times during the week. A woman experienced in ESO usually begins extended orgasm with brief sex almost as soon as her partner's penis enters her vagina. Her partner's state of arousal will also be higher; he will feel more pleasure more quickly and his orgasm will last longer because her strong, continuous contractions stimulate his penis. Five-minute sex under these conditions can satisfy both partners. The "quickie" and the "nooner" come into their own.

Interruptions

There are unavoidable interruptions in every couple's sexual life. Holiday activities, visiting relatives, sick children, business travel, personal illness, even the subtle cycles of individual sexual intensity may interrupt your learning. What you have learned won't be lost, any more than the ability to ski or sail or ride a bicycle is lost when it isn't practiced. Your skills will come back to you when you begin again. You may be wobbly at first. You can pick up and go on.

Discuss your schedule with your partner and agree on ample time for learning ESO: two or more half hours during the week and at least an hour and a half on weekends.

Creating Romance

If sex is scheduled, what happens to romance? You need to learn to create it deliberately.

(A word here about being deliberate. This applies to scheduling lovemaking. It applies to creating romance. It applies to ESO training itself: you may feel silly at first, learning all these new structures. Awkward. Self-conscious. Like an actor in a new role who hasn't yet mastered his lines. You feel that way because you're acquiring new skills. You acquire any new skill by working through the procedure deliberately until it begins to be automatic—"natural," as we say. When you're doing something deliberately, you're watching yourself. And watching yourself means, literally, being self-conscious. It's normal. It's necessary to learning. The way to deal with it is to laugh at yourself. Accept the awkwardness and enjoy a temporary vacation from life's burden of dignity. Be supportive of your partner's awkwardness—laugh *with* your partner. There's room for laughter in bed. You're there, after all, to have fun.)

Romance. Some men won't know what that is. Most women will. We wish men and women were equally knowledgeable, but they aren't. That's been our experience as therapists. Someday they will be. For now, by default, women have volunteered to be the keepers of romance. Men usually undervalue it. They've been taught to ignore it and get the job done. In recent years, though, as women have become more assertive, some men have also begun to wish for more romance.

Romance is setting and mood. It's positive attention to each other rather than to outside matters. It's positive feelings and talk rather than negative. It's taking a positive inventory of your partner—discovering, rediscovering, and enjoying your partner's attractive qualities and ignoring for the moment your critical thoughts. It's compliments, looking at one another with appreciation, listening, touching, hugging, holding hands. It's a formal way into intimacy, an arrangement of symbols and cues.

Romance is also—and this may be why so many men distrust it—a tacit request, usually a woman's tacit request, for reassurance. "Before I allow you to enter my body, I would like to know that you value me. I would like you to tell me so. I would like you to show me by giving me your attention, even by praising me and declaring your love, if only for this moment. You will lose yourself in pleasure with the gift of my body and my mouth and my hands; is reassurance too much to ask?"

If you think romance is a waste of time, think again. Paying attention to romance will win your romantic partner's warm attention in return. Isn't that what you want?

Creating romance is a social skill. People who are good at it weren't born that way. They learned. So can you.

Romance is important to ESO training. You're acquiring new skills, but they aren't merely mechanical. They're an enlarging of your experience of intimacy with your partner. They depend on trust and caring. You don't send your genitals alone into the bedroom. All of you is there. All of you must be considered and all of your partner. So communication, setting, and mood are important when you're learning ESO, just as they are at other intimate times. Without them, one or both of you will be distracted or feel used. Neither state is conducive to pleasure.

The way to find out what your partner considers romantic is to ask. The way to let your partner know is to speak up.

We give our clients that advice and they mention mind reading. "He should already know." In fact, the conditions that encourage someone to feel warm and sexy are as individually specific as most other human preferences. A fire may seem romantic to one person and boring to another. Tastes in music vary across an enormous range.

One of our clients, Alex, couldn't decide what to give his wife for their sixth wedding anniversary. The year before, he'd taken her out for an expensive dinner. Instead of pleasing her, that had made her cold and withdrawn. We suggested that Alex give Helen a single red rose this time. He was skeptical. We encouraged him and he bought the rose and took it home. The next time we saw Alex he raved. "It's amazing. I gave Helen one rose and she was warm all evening." Helen simply wanted to know that Alex thought of her apart from the normal routines of the day. Alex took *clients* out to dinner. The rose was only for her. That was romantic to Helen, then.

If neither of you is quite sure what you find romantic, think back to when you were dating. People in the early stages of courtship usually pay more attention to romance. Did you take walks together? Hold hands? Talk—share experiences, make each other laugh? Compliment each other more than you do now? Discuss restoring some of these pleasures to your lives.

Longing for romance—for close, loving attention—and sexual frustration can be mixed up together, especially in women. When women are sexually frustrated and miss the positive romantic attention they feel they need, we've found they become withdrawn, depressed, or angry. In a word, irritable. This reaction, which is often unconscious, may lead them to start arguments over issues that are seemingly unrelated. That sounds irrational, but it operates by the logic of frustration: at least their arguing makes their partners pay attention, and better angry attention than none at all.

Partners, especially men, need to be alert enough to read such responses accurately. When a man finds his partner deliberately picking a fight, he should try to give her his positive, romantic, undivided attention and work *slowly* toward lovemaking. Often it's not until after satisfactory sex that a woman (or a man, although we find this syndrome more frequently in women) will recognize the real source of her hostility for what it is—pent-up sexual frustration and a hunger for loving attention. She may not acknowledge those motives, but her partner will still find her to be calmer, less irritable, and ultimately more loving if he pays attention.

Incorporate romance into your daily living. Start in the morning, not ten minutes before sex.

Paying Attention

Most romantic arrangements have in common a space of time and a partner's full positive attention. Attention first of all. Call your partner during the day. Let each other know you care. When you come home from work, after you've allowed yourself half an hour or so for practical matters, sit down and talk. Sit down and listen. Pay more attention to what your partner is saying than to what you want to reply. "What did you do today?" Listen supportively while your partner clears away the day's debris. Until the debris is cleared away, you can't come together emotionally. (For exercises to guide you, see "Communicating," p. 194.)

At such times both of you should emphasize positives, set aside negatives, and postpone discussing problems, unless there's an emergency. You can find other times for criticism, worries, complaints. (Some people don't believe they can control their feelings deliberately. They can. We all do, whenever we're in social situations where anger, for example, is inappropriate. With bosses, for example, or in church. If it's possible to control your feelings among strangers, it's equally possible with the man or woman you love.) Imagine you're beginning an evening or weekend date. Compliment each other. Joke. Tease. Kid. Touch. Have fun together. Lighten your heart. *Care.* Tonight's the night!

Sit down to a romantic dinner. That may mean candlelight and a bottle of wine. It may mean a sandwich out under a tree. It may mean no more—but no less—than husband and wife smiling at each other across a table of children. Eating is a pleasure of its own, one we have shaped to a way of sharing. Eat for the pleasure of the food and pay attention to the partner you're sharing it with.

After dinner you may have to interrupt this pleasant performance you've arranged. Discuss what needs to be done to clear the decks: children put to bed, a telephone call made, a favorite TV show watched, the dog walked. Agree when you'll get back together. Then go ahead and do what you need to do to make possible your space of private, uninterrupted time.

Romantics don't like interruptions. The evening would be smoother without them. But intimacy won't be lost if you both agree to them and know that after they're dealt with, you'll pick up where you left off, and that the goal you're both working toward is clearing time together in privacy to give each other pleasure.

Arranging a Place

We approach the bedroom door (or the living-room floor, or whatever other comfortable space of privacy you've chosen). The room you choose for lovemaking deserves attention.

It ought to be warm enough for nakedness. If turning up the furnace isn't possible, consider buying a space heater that you can use during lovemaking and afterward put away.

Unless you live alone, the room should have a door and the door should have a privacy lock. If it doesn't, install one. Nothing is harder on lovemaking than the sudden appearance in the room of a child who wonders why you're wrestling or a grandmother looking for something to read.

For mood as well as for privacy, you'll probably want a source of pleasant sound. Uninterrupted music is best. A stereo is nice. A radio will serve. Some people like to leave on their TV. That's less satisfactory because picture and sound can distract you from giving your partner your undivided attention.

Sounds that screen may be important to you as you learn ESO, because one of the skills you'll work on is vocalizing your pleasure and you may feel inhibited if you think other people can hear. We encourage couples to moan. If they don't know how, we teach them. They start by practicing deliberately at times when they're not making love. They blush and giggle about it. We teach vocalizing because silence during lovemaking is a learned control that limits pleasure. If you're thinking about not making noise, you're not completely letting go. ESO involves learning to let go completely, learning to abandon yourself to sensation. Silence also often means you're holding your breath. That interferes with reaching orgasm and moving above orgasm to ESO. (For further discussion about vocalizing, see "Learning to Vocalize," p. 207.)

Most people make love on a bed. You may want to provide a special sheet for ESO to protect your sleeping sheets from the lubricants you will use. You don't have to change the sheets. Just put the special sheet on top. There's nothing wrong with making love on the floor, on pillows. Create a nest, a comfortable place. Be deliberate about it.

Be deliberate about light levels, candles, incense if you like incense, and any other special arrangements you enjoy—erotic media such as films, for example. If deliberation still seems foolish, think about the last party you gave. You sent invitations, cleaned house, bought food and drink. You probably showered beforehand and dressed in special clothes you don't wear every day. You adjusted lights, stacked your favorite records on your stereo, set out your better glasses and china and tableware. Your guests arrived.

No one mentioned the special preparations other than to compliment you on them. You forgot about them to have fun. You do the same thing when you create a special setting for lovemaking.

Lighting

Light levels can be a problem if partners disagree. Low, warm light is better than darkness for ESO. Observing each other passionately naked is erotic. And whoever is pleasuring needs to see what he's doing. The eyes of the pleasured partner won't always be open, but the eyes of the partner giving pleasure probably will be. If either of you prefers total darkness during lovemaking, you should both discuss why. Often the reason is self-consciousness about your body. Talk it out. Your partner may not feel the same way you do: "I'm embarrassed about my stretch marks." "I'm glad you told me. I'm not even aware of them. I love your body."

(If you want to work toward adding light comfortably to your lovemaking, you can. See "Adding Light," p. 206.)

Supplies

You should arrange ahead of time any equipment or supplies you want in the room you've chosen for lovemaking—perhaps towels, bathrobes, a carafe of juice or wine or a favorite beverage.

One supply you'll need is a good lubricant. It must be oil-based, not water-based. You will need a lubricant for ESO because you'll be stroking delicate tissues for long periods of time. Natural lubrication, even from women who naturally lubricate extensively during sex, isn't adequate. Neither is saliva. Neither are lotions, creams, jellies, nor any other water-based substances.

We have found two commercial lubricants that serve well for ESO. One is petrolatum, also known as petroleum jelly. The best-known brand of petrolatum is Vaseline. It's a long-lasting lubricant, but it's extremely difficult to wash off and many people find it too greasy. It isn't our first choice, but it will serve.

Unscented Albolene Liquifying Cleanser, a makeup remover, is the best lubricant for ESO. It feels better than petrolatum. Our experience with many hundreds of clients confirms that it is definitely the most sensuous, long-lasting lubricant available. It isn't widely distributed, but if you can possibly find it in your local drugstore, do not substitute any other type of lubricant. In contact with skin, it melts to the consistency of natural sexual lubrication but is longer-lasting. It is also completely tasteless, for those times when you proceed from manual to oral stimulation. Even people who at first resist using a lubricant find that the experience of using Albolene usually changes their doubts into appreciation.

If Albolene isn't available, one practical solution is to make your own lubricant. Use the following basic recipe.

> 20 tablespoons mineral oil
> 4 tablespoons melted paraffin
> 2 tablespoons melted petrolatum

> Heat to boiling an inch of water in a large saucepan. Set petrolatum in its store container in the boiling water to melt and measure 2 tablespoons into a small saucepan. Melt chunks of paraffin in a second small saucepan or bowl set in the boiling water and measure into the saucepan that contains the measured petrolatum. Set the saucepan with the paraffin/petrolatum mixture into the boiling water and add the mineral oil. Stir to thoroughly mix. While liquid, pour mixture into decorative container. Container should have a lid. Allow to cool.

You can scent and flavor this lubricant—or petrolatum or Albolene, for that matter—by adding flavoring oils while it's still liquid. Almond, coconut, lemon, banana, and vanilla are possible flavorings. Be sure the flavoring you use is an oil, not an extract. Extracts are made with alcohol and won't mix. Two or three drops of flavoring oil are enough. Adding oil of cloves produces a slight warming effect that some people enjoy.

(If you're uncomfortable using a lubricant, see "Lubrication," p. 204.)

Fingernails

For ESO, nails need to be trimmed very short and with the corners rounded. It's a minor but important point, a sub-sub-sub-issue under the heading of trust. Unless your nails are short, you'll cause your partner pain. Women who enjoy long fingernails will be sorry to sacrifice them, but short nails are a necessity. At the very least, one finger on a woman's dominant hand must be short-nailed. Two or three short-nailed fingers are preferable. Life is compromise. The benefit in this case is pleasure.

Bathing

Allow time to bathe or shower together before ESO. Our experience as physician and sex therapist confirms that nothing inhibits good sex more than poor hygiene. You've read in other guidebooks that the smells of the belovéd are wonderful, and if they're fresh, they may be. But most Americans are conditioned to thorough cleanliness, especially for oral sex. The way to assure each other that you are clean is to bathe together. At minimum, wash thoroughly with soap and a washcloth.

By bathing together, what could be an interruption becomes a sensual pleasure of its own. Wash each other's genitals—that helps you to know them. Dry each other afterward and enjoy that pleasure too. We recommend douching with warm water (rather than douching preparations) once a week as routine hygiene. Some women will feel more comfortable using a warm-water douche after intercourse so that semen will not drip onto clothing as it otherwise does, even the morning after. If you have a persistent problem with odor or discharge, you should rely on your gynecologist's advice.

Alcohol

We haven't mentioned alcohol. Some people find that it enhances mood and promotes relaxation. Use it, if you both agree, in moderation. Alcohol is an anesthetic, like ether or chloroform. It also causes depression and emotional instability. A man who drinks too much will have serious trouble achieving and maintaining an erection. More than two glasses of wine or beer or two cocktails during any three-hour period before or during lovemaking is probably too much. Don't delude yourself about alcohol. You'd be surprised how many people do.

Marijuana

Marijuana alters the perception of time. For some users, time seems to pass more slowly than usual. Pleasurable feelings may seem prolonged. Marijuana also helps some people focus their attention on feelings rather than thoughts.

On the other hand, frequent—daily—marijuana use has been proven in authoritative scientific studies to lower androgens, which are the main hormones determining the level of sex drive—libido—in both men and women. Low androgens in men not only diminish interest in sex, they also adversely affect erection and ejaculation. Daily marijuana use—even two "joints" a day—appears to produce as much lung damage as a pack of cigarettes. Also, among some users, marijuana can cause anxiety and paranoia.

Finally, although vast numbers of people have sampled it, marijuana is illegal.

You will have to decide if the benefits of using marijuana outweigh the serious disadvantages. If you decide for marijuana, don't use it every time you have sex. *ESO produces a natural high that is far better than any drug-induced high.* A prolonged state of orgasm stimulates your production of sex hormones. It also seems to increase the pleasurable levels of your body's own natural narcotic, endorphin.

Anger

We enter the bedroom. One final caution: leave anger outside. Even if you're angry. If you've agreed to come together with your partner for lovemaking, give up anger while you do. Lovemaking isn't a time for criticism, for complaint, for nagging, least of all for anger. If you're feeling angry, imagine gathering your anger together and stuffing it into a plastic garbage bag. Close the bag with a twist tie. Set it outside the bedroom door. You can pick it up in half an hour. Maybe the garbage man will tiptoe up to the door while you're inside, giving and taking pleasure, and carry your garbage away. (If anger continues to be a problem, see "Communicating," p. 194.)

The scene is set. You'll soon forget the props. You're ready to begin. The seventeenth-century English poet John Donne knew how miraculous that beginning can feel:

> And now good morrow to our waking souls,
> Which watch not one another out of fear;
> For love, all love of other sights controls,
> And makes one little room, an everywhere. . . .

III

DEVELOPING SKILLS

What You Should Know About Anatomy

To give pleasure you need to understand your partner's sexual anatomy. To take pleasure you need to understand your own. We also want to identify the parts and responses we'll be talking about later. Some you'll know. Others may not be familiar. Some of our information is new. Here's a brief review.

Female Anatomy

We'll discuss the female anatomy first.

FEMALE ANATOMY

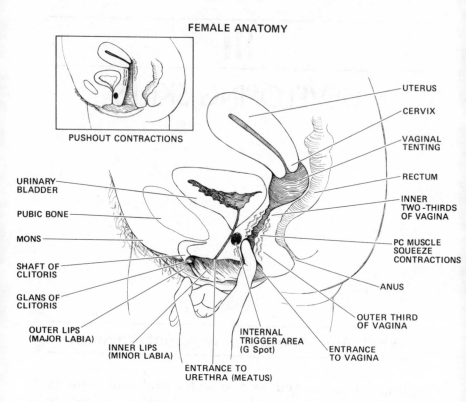

PUSHOUT CONTRACTIONS

URINARY BLADDER

PUBIC BONE

MONS

SHAFT OF CLITORIS

GLANS OF CLITORIS

OUTER LIPS (MAJOR LABIA)

INNER LIPS (MINOR LABIA)

ENTRANCE TO URETHRA (MEATUS)

INTERNAL TRIGGER AREA (G Spot)

ENTRANCE TO VAGINA

UTERUS

CERVIX

VAGINAL TENTING

RECTUM

INNER TWO-THIRDS OF VAGINA

PC MUSCLE SQUEEZE CONTRACTIONS

ANUS

OUTER THIRD OF VAGINA

The major labia normally rest closed over the other parts of the female genitals, protecting them. *Labia* means "lips." That's more or less what they look like under their protective padding of hair. When a woman becomes sexually excited, her major labia expand and flatten against her groin, opening her genitals and exposing their sensitive inner structures.

The minor labia also normally rest closed. With sexual excitement they lengthen and thicken until they protrude well past the major labia. When a woman approaches orgasm, the minor labia change color, depending on skin color and how many children a woman has had, to bright red or even to a deep wine.

The clitoris, with its glans, its hood, and its shaft, appears at the upper junction of the minor labia. When a woman is sexually stimulated, the glans clitoris enlarges at least enough to smooth out the wrinkles in its covering of skin. In a minority of women the glans may enlarge up to double its normal size. However little or much it swells, its changes follow along with the changes in the length and thickness of the minor labia. As a woman reaches high levels of sexual arousal and approaches orgasm, the entire body of the clitoris—glans and shaft—retracts inward and down toward the vagina, until the glans is entirely hidden under the clitoral hood. If arousal then decreases, the clitoris reappears. If arousal increases again, the clitoris retracts again.

Downward from the clitoris and within the shelter of the major and minor labia is the small opening of the urethra. The urethra is the tube that leads outward from the bladder and carries away urine.

Downward from the urethral opening is the opening of the vagina. The vagina serves for sexual intercourse and for birth. Normally the vagina is collapsed upon itself so that its walls are touching all along its length. A woman's first physical response to sexual stimulation is vaginal lubrication. The walls of the vagina produce lubricating fluid by a process similar to sweating.

With continuing arousal the vagina opens and lengthens. It produces more lubrication. The uterus—the womb—elevates inside the body, making a tentlike space above the bottom of the vaginal barrel. At the same time the outer third of the vaginal barrel becomes congested with blood and actually closes down smaller than its previous opening which allows it to hold and to feel a penis of any size, from very small to very large.

With the beginning of brief orgasm the outer third of the vagina pulses in rhythmic contraction. This pulsing is the work of a sling of muscle, the pubococcygeus (*pyub*-oh-cock-sih-*gee*-us), that attaches to the pubic bone in front and the coccyx or tailbone in back. The P.C. muscle surrounds the opening of the urethra and the vagina. It's an important muscle to get to know. We'll discuss it after we describe the male's sexual anatomy.

Locating the Inner Trigger—the G Spot

An important and little-known feature of female anatomy is an area in the vagina that in many women can help function as an orgasmic trigger. It's not usually sensitive nor even palpable except at high levels of sexual excitement. Some sexually experimental couples have known for years of an inner trigger area, but it was first mentioned in the professional literature some thirty years ago by a gynecologist, Dr. Ernest Grafenberg. And only in the past several years have sex therapists appreciated the important role this area can serve in the orgasmic process.

It's variously called "the twelve o'clock spot," the "inner trigger," the "Grafenberg spot," or the "G spot." It's an area of tissue in the upper front wall of the vagina, varying in size from shirt-button to coat-button, just behind the pubic bone, which is the bone you can feel above and toward the front of the vagina. The G-spot trigger area is located on the vaginal wall about one and a half to two inches in depth at the twelve o'clock position. Sometimes it's more toward the eleven- or one-o'clock position.

It normally can't be easily felt. The best time to locate it is immediately after a woman has had orgasm. It is then already somewhat enlarged and sensitive. If a partner presses the G-spot trigger area with one or two fingers and strokes it at a rate of about once a second, a woman mentally open to the experience will usually become more sexually aroused. Experiment with alternating lighter and firmer pressure. Be guided by your partner's response.

The next-best time to locate the G spot is when a woman is near orgasm. If her partner continues clitoral stimulation manually or orally, when he identifies and strokes the G spot she may crest over into orgasm.

Pressure on the G spot may feel uncomfortable at first. It may produce an urge to urinate. That's not a sign that a partner should stop stimulating the area. He should simply lighten his stroke. After a minute or so of continued pressure and stroking, discomfort usually gives way to pleasure.

With continued stroking, the G spot increases in size, hardens—much as the clitoris and penis do—and is then easier to locate.

What exactly is this inner trigger area? There are several theories. It may be sensitive because nerves from the clitoris pass through it on their way to the spinal cord. It may be an area surrounding the female urethra which contains a vestigial prostate gland. Gynecologists and pathologists agree that the area does contain some paraurethral ducts that are similar to the male prostate, and as we will discuss later, stimulating the male prostate helps to trigger a deeper male orgasm in many men.

One research team—Ladas, Whipple, and Perry—even reports that stimulating this spot can cause a small percentage of women to ejaculate a fluid that is chemically similar to seminal fluid. As *ESO* goes to press, we know of no other researchers who have confirmed by chemical analysis the existence of a female ejaculate.

But regardless of whether or not females ejaculate, locating the internal trigger area at about the twelve-o'clock position in the upper wall of the vagina is important for women who wish to experience ESO. Later on we'll explain how to do so.*

*Very occasionally we have encountered women who develop a bladder infection called cystitis when they are beginning to learn about G-spot stimulation. This is easily treated with antibiotics such as Gantrasin and usually does not occur again. It may be like "honeymoon cystitis," which occurs once or twice in some brides and other women who begin sexual activity after a period of sexual inactivity. It can be annoying, but it is not dangerous.

A woman who is unable to locate the G spot will still very possibly discover an area in her vagina that is especially sensitive. Usually this area is located along the front wall of the vagina, but sensitivity may occur instead at other positions. Careful attention to the sex exploration exercises we will be discussing—both partners' attention—can help with identifying a vaginal area or areas that respond pleasurably to stimulation. Later, when we talk about stimulating the G spot, women who have located other areas of vaginal sensitivity should direct stimulation there instead.

Male Anatomy

Next, look at the male sexual anatomy.

MALE ANATOMY

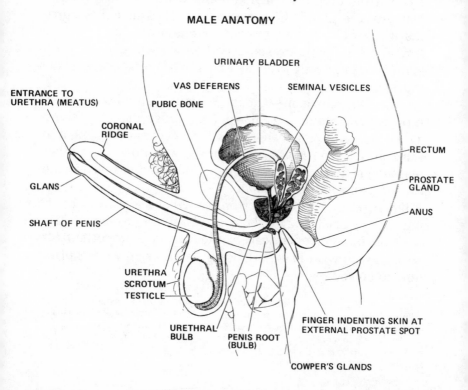

The male penis in its unaroused state is a short, soft tube of spongy tissue that provides a channel for emptying the bladder of urine. The male urethra runs along the length of the underside of the penis. The penis itself is not a muscle and contains no muscles, nor any bones. Two to three inches of it is rooted inside the body in the pubococcygeus musculature. Specific exercises can strengthen that musculature and thus help make erections harder. (See p. 55, "Advanced Techniques.")

In males who haven't been circumcised, the head of the penis—the glans—is covered by a loose tube of skin called the foreskin. Circumcised males have had their foreskins surgically removed, leaving their glans permanently exposed.

The penis erects with sexual stimulation. Valves close down in veins that would normally return to the body the blood carried to the penis by its arteries. The organ increases in length and thickness as its spongy tissue fills with blood.

With increasing arousal the glans swells to several times its unaroused state and sometimes darkens in color. Erection occurs in newborn baby boys as well as in men ninety years old. It occurs a number of times every night during sleep in every healthy male. Erection is a man's first physical response to sexual stimulation, as lubrication is a woman's. At ejaculation, semen spurts from the urethral opening in the penis with enough force to propel itself outward several inches, sometimes a foot or more.

Aroused or unaroused, different penises vary greatly in thickness and length. The size differences are largely hereditary. They don't correlate with body size. A large man may have a small penis; a small man may have a large penis. Penises do tend to withdraw into the body with lack of sexual use, as some sexually inactive older men have discovered. Some men experienced in ESO have reported some permanent increase in the length of their penises—up to an inch. This increase may come from those several inches of buried treasure rooted inside the body. Frequent erection, prolonged erection, and maximum erection, all part of ESO, stimulate the penis over a period of months to enlarge to its maximum length and thickness. Further stimulation comes from the exercises we'll be recommending to strengthen the P.C. muscle and muscles at the penile base and from the stimulation techniques of ESO itself. A man can track changes in penile length during ESO training by measuring his erect penis along the top, from pubic bone to tip. If penis size is a concern of yours or of your partner's, this increase could be a fringe benefit of learning ESO.

In our experience, most men overemphasize the value of a large penis. The great majority of women count many other qualities in a man more important than the size of his penis. And couples who regularly experience ESO, in particular, enjoy such high levels of sexual satisfaction and such correspondingly high levels of sexual self-confidence that any concern they may once have had about penis size becomes minimal.

Below and behind the penis is the scrotum. The scrotum is a sac of skin that contains the testicles, the two walnut-size glands where sperm are nurtured. The scrotum, and the two cords that support the testicles, raise and lower the testicles against and away from the body to regulate their temperature. Sperm die if they're kept at body temperature for very long, which is why the wives of men who wear tight undershorts sometimes have difficulty getting pregnant.

With sexual arousal a man's testicles swell, sometimes doubling or even tripling in size. Along with the thickened, engorged scrotum, they draw up against his body as he approaches orgasm. Men usually can't ejaculate until their testicles are fully drawn up against their bodies.*

Behind the scrotum, toward the anus, and inside the body

---

*Men under fifty. Men over fifty may not experience full elevation of both testicles. Some men with low-hanging testicles find that although their scrotum lifts, it never actually pulls the testicles against the body.

is a gland known as the prostate. It surrounds the male urethra inside the body directly in front of the urinary bladder. It supplies part of the clear fluid that bathes the swimming sperm that the testicles produce and that is expelled from the body at ejaculation.

The prostate in the male, like the G spot in the female, is often highly sensitive to stimulation, especially when there is already excitement with erection. A man's sexual arousal can be increased simply by massaging his prostate with a finger inserted through the anus into the rectum. The prostate can also be stimulated less directly—but more easily and comfortably—by applying pressure behind the scrotum to the area between the back of the scrotum and the anus, in the valley of skin known as the perineum (pear-ih-*nee*-um). We call this important pressure point the *external prostate spot*. Not every man finds this stimulation arousing at first. The closer a man is to orgasm, the more likely he is to find prostate stimulation pleasurable.

There is some evidence that men who go through life with a low frequency of orgasm are more likely to suffer from prostate enlargement and prostatic cancer than men who are sexually more active.

A man in an advanced state of sexual arousal will often secrete a drop or two of clear fluid from the opening of his penis prior to orgasm and ejaculation. This preseminal fluid heralds the approach of the emission phase of orgasm.

Similarities

Male and female sexual anatomy look dramatically different, and they are—one is almost the reverse of the other—but in terms of how the genitals develop, they're very much alike. The male and female genitals evolve from the same tissues in the developing fetus. Look at the illustration

"Comparable Male-Female Structures," which shows the male and female genitals side by side.

COMPARABLE MALE–FEMALE STRUCTURES

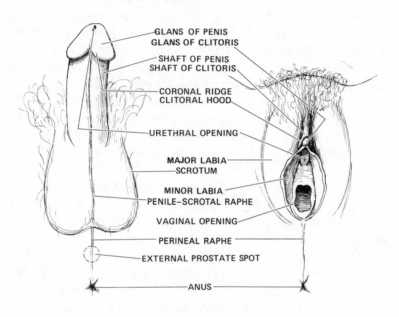

GLANS OF PENIS
GLANS OF CLITORIS
SHAFT OF PENIS
SHAFT OF CLITORIS
CORONAL RIDGE
CLITORAL HOOD
URETHRAL OPENING
MAJOR LABIA
SCROTUM
MINOR LABIA
PENILE–SCROTAL RAPHE
VAGINAL OPENING
PERINEAL RAPHE
EXTERNAL PROSTATE SPOT
ANUS

The male scrotum and the female major labia develop from the same fetal tissue. The shaft of the penis and the shaft of the clitoris correspond. So, most importantly, do the glans penis and the glans clitoris. Remember these similarities when you stimulate your partner. They'll help you understand where your partner is sensitive and how that sensitivity feels.

The similarity between the glans penis and the glans clitoris partly explains why many women don't have orgasm during ordinary intercourse. When a man's penis is thrusting in a woman's vagina, he's directly stimulating his most sensitive organ but only indirectly stimulating hers. Only about one woman in three is orgasmic with intercourse. That's another reason why ESO, which involves direct clitoral stimulation (and direct penile stimulation), is more pleasurable than intercourse alone.

Jeff, the boyfriend of one of our clients, learned about clitoral stimulation the hard way. Angie almost moved out. They're thirty-five and thirty-three years old. Angie works in an office, Jeff in construction. Angie came to see us because she expected to be transferred to another state soon and wasn't sure she wanted Jeff to go along. She was extremely angry with him, partly because he wasted all his money and some of hers on drugs, partly because he made love to her vigorously but inattentively. She'd been orgasmic with other partners before she met Jeff. They'd been orgasmic together at first. Now she rarely had orgasm. She would passively lie back without actively participating in intercourse. She felt that Jeff had stopped caring about her pleasure and was concerned only about his own.

We worked to improve their whole relationship. Included in that work was straightforward training in manual stimulation and in taking turns giving and receiving pleasure. Within three weeks Angie started having orgasm again. After ten therapy sessions she learned to extend her orgasm to three minutes at a time. Jeff also learned to extend his orgasm. The quality of their intercourse changed wonderfully. For that and other reasons their entire relationship improved. When Angie's job transfer came through, she enthusiastically encouraged Jeff to join her. He did. Angie wrote us later that she has had some orgasms with Jeff that have lasted five to ten minutes.

Differences

One more comment about anatomy: each of us is different, from our unique fingerprints and the unique sizes and responses of our genitals to our unique patterns of orgasm. "There is nothing more characteristic of the sexual response," the pioneer sex researcher Alfred Kinsey concluded after interviewing thousands of men and women, "than the fact that it is not the same in any two individuals." That's because the body's central organ of sexual response is the brain.

Some women can stimulate themselves to orgasm by caressing only their breasts; others cannot. Some men and women experience a red, rashlike flush on their upper bodies with orgasm; others do not. Some men stop thrusting at the onset of orgasm; others continue thrusting until orgasm is concluded. There are patterns common to all, and there is much of sensation and pleasure that can be learned. It's worth remembering always that your partner is first of all an individual, is first of all a human being, and is more like you than different—concerning problems as well as pleasures.

Kegel Exercises

Even knowledgeable men and women who have heard of the great value of developing the special sex muscles usually have not bothered to train them. For increased sexual pleasure we strongly advise all our clients to develop their sexual muscles (the pubococcygeus or P.C. muscles). You may not know that you do, but you probably use your P.C. muscle to increase sexual arousal during intercourse. The stronger your P.C., the more control you have over its action. The better exercised it is, the greater the flow of stimulating blood in the genitals. Weight lifters find pleasure "pumping up" their muscles by exercising them at the beginning of a workout, causing them to enlarge and fill with blood. Working your P.C. similarly adds pleasure during sexual stimulation.

P.C. exercise is extremely important to successful ESO.

Back in the late 1940s a gynecologist named Dr. Arnold Kegel (pronounced *Kay*-gill) developed a good, basic program of P.C. exercises to help women who have problems controlling their bladders. It's clear now that "Kegel exercises" work equally well for men and condition the P.C. for sexual arousal.

Here's how a woman can identify her P.C. muscle:

Sit on a toilet. Spread your legs apart. See if you can stop and start the flow of urine without moving your legs. The muscle you use to do that, the one that turns the flow on and off, is your P.C. muscle. If you don't find it the first time, don't give up. Try again the next time you have to urinate.

And here's how a man can identify his P.C.:

Try to stop the flow of urine during urination. The muscle you use is your P.C. You may feel a tightening around your anus as well. You also use your P.C. to bear down to force out the last drops of urine.

Kegel exercises are simple three-part exercises:

> *Slow Clenches:* Squeeze and clench the P.C. muscle as you did to stop the flow of urine. Hold for a slow count of three. Relax.
>
> *Flutters:* Clench and relax the P.C. as quickly as you can.
>
> *Push-outs:* Women: bear down moderately as if trying to have a bowel movement or as if in labor. Men: bear down moderately as if you're forcing out urine or a bowel movement. Men and women: this exercise will

use a number of stomach (abdominal) muscles as well as the P.C. muscle. You'll also feel your anus tightening and relaxing.

Begin training your P.C. by doing ten Slow Clenches, ten Flutters, and ten Push-outs (that's one *set*) five times every day.

After a week, add five Slow Clenches, five Flutters, and five Push-outs to each set and continue doing five sets a day.

After another week, add five more of each exercise and continue doing five sets a day.

Add five of each exercise each week until a set includes thirty of each exercise. Then continue doing at least five sets a day permanently to maintain muscle tone. You should faithfully practice at least 150 Kegel exercises every day once you've trained up to that level.

You can do Kegel exercises almost anywhere—when you're driving, walking, watching TV, doing dishes, sitting at a desk, lying in bed.

When you start exercising, you may find that your P.C. doesn't want to stay tightened during Slow Clenches. You may not be able to do Flutters very quickly or evenly. That's because the muscle is weak. Control improves with practice.

If your P.C. feels tired in the middle of a set, give it a few seconds' rest and then continue.

To feel the contractions of her P.C. muscle and check on its increasing strength, a woman can insert one or two lubricated fingers into her vagina while exercising.

Holding an object in her vagina during P.C. exercise can speed progress toward strength and control. Other than fingers, a woman may use a penis-shaped vibrator. Switching on the vibrator can add pleasurable sensations to the exercise.

Kegel exercises help men develop stronger erections. Learning to tighten, to relax, and to push out the P.C. muscle allows a man to control his sexual system the way he controls a car. *Tightening* is the accelerator, increasing arousal. *Pushing out* is the brake—it can help stop ejaculation.

Remember to breathe naturally and evenly while you're doing Kegel exercises. Do one hundred to two hundred contractions (when you've trained yourself up to that level) faithfully every day. They'll help you with ESO.

Testicle Elevations

These more advanced exercises are obviously for men. It isn't crucial to learn these techniques to achieve ESO, but they help. We'll address men directly in this section.

We said earlier that men can't ejaculate until their testicles are elevated close against their bodies. Cocking a gun is a good analogy. The gun won't go off unless the hammer is pulled back. Similarly, unless your testicles elevate, you don't ejaculate. If you learn to elevate and to lower your testicles voluntarily, you gain control over an important automatic function. That control increases your erection strength and degree of arousal. Alternatively, it delays ejaculation. Learning to delay ejaculation is a crucial part of learning male ESO.

Voluntary elevation of the testicles may seem difficult at first. It takes time to learn to identify the specific muscles involved. Initially you'll need to tighten all the lower abdominal muscles to raise your testicles. Later, with practice, you'll be able to raise them using only the appropriate pelvic muscles without tensing the abdominal muscles at all.

It's also difficult at first to feel the testicles moving up and down. Use a mirror to help you see what's happening. Even better, ring your scrotum above your testicles with thumb and middle finger and gently pull down. Then you'll be able to feel a slight movement of your testicles when you correctly contract and relax the internal muscles that control their elevation.

Once you locate the right muscles, practice raising and lowering your testicles until you can quickly do so one hundred times in succession. Practice this exercise either sitting at the edge of a chair or standing with your feet spaced about eighteen inches apart. Practice elevating your testicles both with and without an erection, while you are stimulating yourself and while you are being stimulated by your partner.

Physical Exercise

ESO is energetic, but it isn't strenuous. You don't have to be an athlete to learn it and to do it well. On the other hand, better physical conditioning will improve your ability to give your partner pleasure and to take pleasure yourself.

So, besides Kegel exercises and other specifically sexual exercises, we recommend that both men and women follow a regular program of at least moderate overall physical conditioning. Depending upon your age, your present condition, and your general health, such a program may include jogging, bicycling, walking, jumping rope, doing push-ups, sit-ups, calisthenics, group or individual exercise, or swimming.

If physical exercise is to be of any value to you, you must do it regularly—at least three times a week. But exercise sessions don't have to be long. Even five or ten minutes of moderate calisthenics or exercise against resistance can make a large difference in your physical stamina and sense of well-being within a month or two.

A recent study by James White of the University of California at San Diego compared middle-aged men who followed a prescribed exercise program three hours a week for nine months with a group of similar men who didn't exercise. The exercise group had significantly more sexual drive, arousal, and orgasms.

Note that upper-body exercises, particularly arm exercises that work the bicep and tricep muscles, can give a man more endurance for prolonged manual stimulation of his partner's clitoris and vagina. So, too, a woman in better physical condition will find it easier and more comfortable to stimulate her partner at length and vigorously.

You don't have to become a body builder. You don't have to pump iron. But you'll feel better and have more pleasure sexually if you practice at least moderate physical conditioning for a total of at least fifteen or twenty minutes a week.

Self-Stimulation

Training in self-stimulation is a basic preparation for ESO. You may know self-stimulation by another name. The old medical term, derived from an obscure Latin word, is *masturbation*. Another and uglier term for self-stimulation is self-abuse.

Self-stimulation doesn't cause insanity, warts, acne, blindness, criminality, homosexuality, ulcers, epilepsy, addiction, or hairy palms. It does help you learn how to achieve sexual arousal and—for men—ejaculatory control. It's a major sexual learning tool because it puts you completely in charge of your stimulation. You can find out what feels good without worrying about your partner at the same time. Even if you have a good sexual relationship with a loving partner, you will benefit from going back to basics, and so will he or she.

Some men and women feel strongly inhibited from self-stimulation because of religious training. For discussion of that problem, see "Religious Prohibitions," p. 142, in Chapter VIII, "Overcoming Resistances."

We treat clients with many different sexual problems. Self-stimulation training is important to that treatment. Even though our clients come to us for help, they often resist stimulating themselves when we advise it. Fear blocks the way.

Bruce was a thirty-four-year-old salesman who complained he wasn't interested in sex. He drank too much and spent too much time in bed—alone, unfortunately. He didn't have a girl friend. He didn't have many other friends either. He hadn't self-stimulated in more than three years.

He protested the self-stimulation training we assigned him. He said it was silly. We insisted. He didn't even have to have an erection, we told him. He only had to self-stimulate thirty minutes a day, three times a week.

For two weeks Bruce complained that the self-stimulation wasn't working. When it didn't work, he said, he stopped doing it: what was the point? That was Bruce's way of sabotaging his progress, but we continued to insist that he follow our program and report his accomplishments.

Three weeks in, Bruce began having erections with self-stimulation. We suggested Kegel exercises, encouraged him to talk about his fantasies, and taught him ways to relax. By the seventh week of treatment he was self-stimulating to orgasm every day. He was drinking less. His energy was returning.

Bruce stopped therapy after three months. By then he was having successful sexual encounters with women. He returned two months later with a girl friend he was serious about. He wanted to learn ESO. Five months before, Bruce had claimed he didn't even think about sex. Self-stimulation training precipitated the dramatic change.

Anna, the forty-seven-year-old wife of a computer company executive, had an equally dramatic success with self-stimulation. Her husband, Gary, convinced her to see us after a suicide gesture (she'd taken several sleeping pills, but not a lethal dose). We learned that she had suffered periodic depressions for many years that long-term psychotherapy had only marginally improved and that antidepressant drugs didn't budge. We also learned that she had never been orgasmic and didn't practice self-stimulation. She and Gary made love several times a month, two or three minutes at a time.

Anna thought very little of herself. We worked to improve her self-esteem. We also started her self-stimulating. Like Bruce, but for different reasons, she resisted. Bruce was afraid of failing. Anna didn't like herself. We asked her to begin simply by looking at herself in a mirror and finding her good points. We asked her to start a program of Kegel exercises.

Eventually Anna learned to have orgasm with self-stimulation, using her hand. "I never thought I could," she told us. "I'm actually beginning to look forward to my private sex time."

Self-stimulation was only a beginning for Anna and Gary. We worked with both of them to help them learn longer and more pleasurable lovemaking. Five months after starting therapy, Anna was no longer depressed. She is now reliably orgasmic with intercourse and with oral and manual stimulation. She occasionally self-stimulates to orgasm. She and Gary make love once or twice a week, and sometimes Anna initiates that lovemaking. We noticed especially an outward change that mirrored Anna's inward improvement. Before therapy, she wore dark colors and matronly clothes. Now she dresses stylishly in colors as cheerful as she has come to feel.

Taking Pleasure

Once you decide to begin ESO training, plan to set aside at least the first two weeks for concentrating on self-stimulation. During that time you may also continue lovemaking with your partner. You may need to devote more than two weeks to self-stimulation exercises, depending on what you learn about your response. If so, continue your usual love-making through that period as well.

Three times during these first two weeks, set aside at least thirty minutes of private time—not secret, private—for self-stimulation. Let your partner know, but spend this time alone. Your purpose is to learn to give yourself pleasure or to review your skills. Then you'll know how to teach your partner.

Pamper yourself. Take a sensuous shower or bath and notice the pleasant feeling of warm water on your skin. Afterward spend some time looking at your body and appreciating its good features. Be as positive and friendly with yourself as you try to be with your partner when you're creating a mood of romance.

Touch your body. Explore it for pleasure—kneading muscles, massaging scalp, caressing skin. Men especially may feel embarrassed caressing themselves. Do it anyway to learn what feels good, even if you think you already know. Many men are almost entirely focused on genital stimulation. They can increase their levels of pleasure enormously by widening their focus to include their entire bodies—scalp, head, face, neck, arms, hands, nipples, chest, back, belly, buttocks, thighs, calves, and feet.

At some point during this time of touching and self-exploration, move to a comfortable place where you can sit or lie down—on a chair, on pillows on the floor, or lying in bed. When you've touched your body for pleasure for at least five minutes, start to explore your genitals. Even if you're familiar with self-stimulation, approach your genitals as if you're doing so for the first time. Don't fall immediately into a practiced pattern. Really *notice* what you're doing, what you're discovering and how it feels.

After a while, add lubrication and notice the difference between dry stimulation and stimulation with a lubricant.

Now we'll discuss men and women separately, beginning with men. Both of you should read both discussions.

Self-Stimulation for Men

Basic Techniques

The basic requirements for effective self-stimulation are (1) ample time, (2) P.C. and pelvic muscle strengthening and control, and (3) paying attention to sensation.

Begin, then, by lubricating not only your penis but also your scrotum and perineum. (If you're uncomfortable using a lubricant, see "Lubrication," p. 204.) Now proceed to stimulate yourself to erection. (If you find it difficult or impossible to achieve an erection with self-stimulation, see "Sexual Problems," p. 170.)

Stimulate yourself to erection and then see if you can keep that erection with self-stimulation and without ejaculation for at least thirty minutes. During that thirty minutes, see if you can bring yourself close to orgasm at least six times. Stop your stroking or reduce speed and pressure each time you near the "point of no return" (ejaculatory inevitability).

If at any time you lose control and ejaculate, enjoy the orgasm, wait awhile, then begin stimulation again. You'll find control easier with sexual tension reduced.

If you're used to quick self-stimulation, you may find that sustaining an erection without orgasm for thirty minutes is difficult at first. You may want to start with only that goal. Then at later sessions add progressively more near-orgasm peaks during the thirty minutes.

Experiment with different kinds of strokes. Most men stimulate themselves with a basic up-and-down stroke of one hand. Some men stimulate themselves by rolling their penis in two hands. Your hand can be turned thumb-up or thumb-down; you can make a ring of your thumb and forefinger; you can concentrate stimulation on the shaft or the glans; you can use both hands and stroke from mid-shaft outward in both directions at once, toward the glans and toward the base; you can press your penis against your belly and rub its underside with the flat of your palm; you can change hands; and these are only a few of the many possible variations. Each time you stimulate yourself is a new experience, because you have added your previous experience to the total of what you know and feel. Your goal is not to ejaculate but to *feel more*—to enjoy the process. If you pay attention to sensation, you won't be bored. Boredom is a form of resistance. If self-stimulation is boring, see Chapter VIII, "Overcoming Resistances."

We once treated an athletic young man named Patrick who stimulated himself by hanging from a chinning bar and banging his erect penis against a door frame. Having conditioned himself to such violent sensations, Patrick wasn't able to enjoy orgasm any other way. That didn't bother him so long as he was unattached, but then he met a girl. Jenny wasn't anything at all like a door frame. Patrick and Jenny had a problem. We helped them solve it by developing a program of gradual deconditioning. Patrick went back to subtler sensations. First we instructed him to use his own hands vigorously and have an ejaculation. Then Jenny added her hand to his. Then he learned to have orgasm and ejaculate with the stimulation of Jenny's hands alone. Then Patrick learned to insert himself into Jenny's vagina just before ejaculation. Before long he was able to enjoy normal intercourse.

When you have achieved hard erection and sustained it for at least five minutes, continue stroking your penis while stimulating your external prostate spot and controlling ejaculation with the scrotal pull technique, which we will explain shortly.

Prostate stimulation involves pressing upward firmly on the perineum, between the anus and the back of the scrotum, with one or more fingers. You may not be familiar with the sensation. Explore it with an open mind. The first stage of orgasm, the emission phase, involves automatic contractions of the prostate. Firm, rhythmic pressure on the prostate, even from outside the body, partly duplicates these sensations of first-stage orgasm. But because you aren't stimulating the ejaculatory reflex, the orgasmic contractions proceed without ejaculation.

If you find it awkward to stimulate your external prostate spot with your left hand (assuming you are right-handed and have been using your dominant hand to stimulate your penis), switch hands and stroke your penis with your left hand while you search out and rhythmically press your external prostate spot with your right. Because this spot is located behind the base of the penis, which is buried inside the body, pressing on it firmly pushes extra blood into your penis, which then should swell and pleasurably throb.

When you find yourself approaching orgasm, one good way to control ejaculation is simply to stop stroking. Use this "stop-start" method first to see how it works. Alternatively you can press firmly on the external prostate spot, which can help reduce the ejaculatory reflex and which many men also find pleasurable.

Still another way to achieve ejaculatory control is scrotal pulling. Pulling your testicles away from your body prevents you from ejaculating. Try it.

To apply the scrotal pull, grasp the scrotum between your testicles with the thumb and forefinger of your left hand. When you're near orgasm, pull firmly down. At other times, for stimulation, pull lightly in rhythm as you stroke. Become thoroughly familiar with the scrotal pull. You'll need to teach it to your partner for ESO.

Another way is to make a ring with your left thumb and forefinger between your testicles and body and pull downward (see illustration number 6 inset for a partner-assisted version of the scrotal pull).

We sometimes have a man use an adjustable cloth or

leather snap ring around his scrotum above his testicles to help him learn the effects of scrotal pulling. Such a ring applies constant pressure, which many men find arousing, and can aid in controlling ejaculation. It should never be adjusted so tightly that it cuts off circulation.

As part of your self-stimulation exercises, you should practice voluntary testicle elevation and lowering, which we discussed earlier. Nearing ejaculation, deliberately relax the muscles that hold your testicles close to your body and notice the effect. You may find the muscular control difficult at first, and the effect may seem too subtle to notice. Keep practicing. After the ejaculatory urge has subsided somewhat, resume stimulating your penis with your hand and at the same time deliberately elevate your testicles. Notice the subtle effect of increasing arousal.

When you've trained yourself to maintain hard, pleasurable erection without orgasm for at least fifteen minutes, go on to half an hour. Once you can sustain arousal for thirty minutes without ejaculating, you will be able to sustain it for as long as you want. Thirty minutes is a necessary minimum to build up the muscular tension and vasocongestion that is essential for ESO. (If you have trouble delaying ejaculation, see "Early Ejaculation," p. 180.)

It may take you longer than two weeks to learn how to prolong erection without ejaculation. If so, continue self-stimulation exercises until you do before going on to ESO training with your partner. *At minimum you should be able to delay ejaculation with self-stimulation for at least thirty minutes before you begin ESO training with your partner.* If you haven't learned to maintain ejaculatory control yourself, how can you teach someone else to do it for you?

If you usually use erotic media—magazines, films, videotapes—during self-stimulation, continue to do so now. If you've never done so, you may want to try, to see if they add to arousal.

A vibrator is another good form of stimulation to add. It's

especially good for applying stimulation externally to the prostate. (For a discussion of types of vibrators, see "Vibrators," p. 212.)

You may not notice any improvement in your sexual experience the first time you add something new. You need time to become comfortable with new procedures, new sensations, and new props. If you find a vibrator disappointing the first time you use it, for instance, don't give it up. Try it again—try it several more times—experimenting with it at leisure before you pass judgment on its value.

Occasionally, when you've stimulated yourself to a high level of arousal, wipe the lubricant off the head of your penis and see if you're secreting clear fluid. Male ESO is marked by such secretions, often in considerable volume—a tablespoon or more. If you produce a few drops during self-stimulation, then you can judge that you're near the beginning of ESO. Notice what you did to get there. ESO itself is possible only with a partner.

Advanced Techniques

(1) *Erection exercises.* Sit on the edge of a chair with your legs spread apart. While you are fully erect, locate the muscles that make your penis throb—that is, that make it get fuller. Locate the muscles that make your penis move up and down, side to side, and back and forth.

Practice moving your penis in these different directions. Practice with your knees together. Practice while squatting and while lying down on your back. You've already begun exercising the muscles involved in making your penis move. They're the P.C. muscles, the abdominal muscles, the buttocks, and the thighs. Notice the effects that contracting single sets and combinations of these muscles have on your penis's movement and on your sensations of pleasure.

Practicing these exercises will increase the strength and hardness of your erection. You can develop further strength by hanging a towel on your erect penis and lifting it. Start with a small face towel and work up to larger, heavier bath towels.

These exercises not only develop extra muscle strength, but also increase the supply of blood to your genitals.

(2) *Repeated ejaculation.* Stimulate yourself without ejaculation for thirty minutes, reward yourself with ejaculation, but then immediately resume stimulating your penis. Instead of becoming soft, it will remain relatively hard. As you continue stimulating it, it will gradually become more erect. You may need to increase the amount of stimulation significantly the second time.

Continue to stimulate yourself for at least another ten minutes. You may experience another ejaculation, with the volume of your ejaculate somewhat reduced. Each time you approach ejaculation, instead of distracting yourself by thinking of other things, pay attention to your penis and to the sensations in your genitals.

(3) *Seminal fluid retention (holding it in).* This exercise is a variation of the repeated-ejaculation exercise. Stimulate yourself without ejaculation for thirty minutes, then increase stimulation. When you feel yourself just beginning to ejaculate, stop stimulating. Take your hands away from your penis, hold your breath, and squeeze your P.C. muscles and your other sexual muscles as tightly as you can. Your goal is to stop completely the ejaculatory fluid from squirting out. If you have trained your P.C. and other sexual muscles, you'll discover that you can retain most of your ejaculate. Surprisingly, though, your orgasm will continue and may even feel stronger.

After your contractions have ceased, resume stimulating yourself. Your erection will probably continue and your arousal will return to a high level. Since you have retained most of your semen, you probably won't have to wait as long as usual before you can have another ejaculation. You may find you can ejaculate again within several minutes. When you do arrive again at the point of ejaculatory inevitability, squeeze down on your P.C. again. Your second orgasm will probably be as strong or stronger than your first.

Notice the amount of fluid you produce in each modified ejaculation. Count the number of internal contractions you experience each time. Compare the number of contractions in your usual orgasm with the number of contractions you experience during these modified procedures.

As you strengthen your sexual muscles and develop control, you may be able to enjoy ten or more separate and distinct orgasms with ejaculation during a single session of self-stimulating. Since you reestablish muscular and vascular tension almost immediately after each modified ejaculation, the cumulative effect is additive: each ejaculation feels a little stronger than the one before. You certainly don't have to try for ten, by the way. Whenever you think you're ready for the final big orgasm, simply let go and enjoy it without holding back any semen.

(4) *Stretching orgasm.* After you've practiced your Kegel and other sexual-muscle exercises for three to four weeks, you'll be ready to begin stretching your orgasms.

Notice how many contractions you feel during a usual ejaculation—normally between three and eight. Once your muscles are toned, you should be able at least to double that number and to reverse their order of intensity. Instead of the strongest contractions coming at the beginning, you can learn to space them further apart and to save the best for the end.

Begin as you began the two preceding exercises with thirty minutes of stimulation. This time, however, as you approach ejaculation, tighten your muscles as you did to hold your ejaculate in, but instead of completely stopping all stimulation, continue stimulating your penis very slowly throughout ejaculation, pushing the sensation on and on, stretching it out for as long as you can sustain it.

Self-Stimulation for Women

As a woman you need to realize first of all that self-stimulation is good for you. It's not a substitute but a supplement. It's healthy. It feels good. It allows you to learn how you like to be pleasured so that you can teach your partner. Best of all, it adds to your orgasmic capacity. The more orgasms you experience, the more you can have.

Every healthy human female is potentially multiorgasmic and is potentially capable of learning to experience ESO. That's your birthright. Why shouldn't you claim it? And the most reliable preparation for ESO is self-stimulation.

Your goal during this preliminary two weeks or more of self-stimulation is different from a man's. He's discovering what feels good. He's also learning to delay orgasm—learning how to hold back. You're discovering what feels good. But you're also learning to *have* orgasm—learning how to let go. If you already know how to have orgasm reliably with self-stimulation, you're learning to extend your capacity, to have several orgasms in a row.

When you've touched your body for pleasure, then, and begun genital exploration, lubricate yourself thoroughly. (If you're uncomfortable using a lubricant, see "Lubrication," p. 204.) Lubricate your major and minor labia, your clitoris, the opening into your vagina, and even a little inside. Lubricate your perineum—the valley of skin between the lower margin of your labia and your anus.

Begin to explore the touch and the stroking you like. First find areas of your genitals that feel good to touch. Then begin touching and stroking those areas for arousal.

If you aren't used to self-stimulation, you may want to pleasure yourself for one or more sessions without trying to achieve orgasm. Later, when you feel you're ready, you can go all the way.

If you're used to self-stimulation, you might spend some time exploring new strokes and touches and pressures. Then go on through orgasm and see if you can give yourself several orgasms in a row.

The object of these self-stimulation exercises is to bring yourself to the point where you can have several orgasms on your own, using only your hands. When you reach that point, you're ready to go on to ESO training with your partner. It may well take more than two weeks. That's fine. You need to learn how to pleasure yourself so you can teach your partner.

Many women today have taught themselves to have orgasm with a vibrator. Vibrators are a godsend, especially in learning about orgasm for the first time, but you can ultimately get more pleasure without a vibrator than with one. If you only self-stimulate with a vibrator, use this preliminary time period to teach yourself to have orgasm by hand.

If you find that you can't achieve orgasm using only your hands, you've encountered a resistance. The way through the resistance is by deconditioning. Give yourself one or more orgasms using your vibrator. Then put it aside and continue to have more orgasms with your hands. At later sessions, put the vibrator aside just before orgasm and use your hands for orgasm itself. Eventually you should be able to stimulate yourself to orgasm without the vibrator. You may still want to use it at other times as a variation you enjoy.

When you can stimulate yourself by hand to several orgasms, then you're ready to begin training with your partner for ESO. (If you are unable to have orgasm with self-stimulation, see "Preorgasmia," p. 185.)

Communicating Sexually

After you've both learned effective self-stimulation, you should move on to sexual communication. You each need to learn how the other likes to be pleasured. The way to do that is first to watch each other and then to teach each other.

We'd suggest you spend at least one session taking turns watching each other self-stimulate. Watch without touching. You can talk or ask questions if you like, but not help.

Then, at the next session, you should take turns mimicking exactly what you saw the other do. Keep that up in additional sessions until you can effectively stimulate your partner, letting your partner be the judge. That may take one session. It may take five or ten. You want to learn at least to equal what your partner can do alone—to equal, at minimum, the best your partner can do with self-stimulation.

This training is instruction. You should each tell each other what's happening and if it's being done right. Guide your partner's hands. Be assertive if you're the one teaching and be accepting if you're the one being taught. Leave anger out of it. Drop your ego. Your partner is the expert, the teacher; you're the novice, the student.

People who have known each other for years, long-married couples, may feel their egos bruising when they train. They may be surprised to learn that they haven't known what their partners really enjoy. Take the lesson for what it is—a chance to give and receive more pleasure than you were giving and receiving before. You'll be loved that much more for accepting the emotional discomfort.

We saw that result with our clients Chris and Myrna, husband and wife for twenty-five years. Chris was a rugged, silent man, a restaurant owner who worked hard. Myrna had to drag him in to see us. He wasn't interested in sex, she said. Chris admitted it. He had trouble achieving erection. "I don't feel like a man," he told us. When they were younger they'd made love two or three times a week; they'd found affection, trust, and friendship together. Now that closeness was fading. Chris accepted the change silently, but Myrna missed what they had shared.

There was hidden anger between Chris and Myrna. There were communication problems and there was an escape into work made easier by the challenge of operating their own business. We concentrated on those problems. But we also helped Chris and Myrna learn to pleasure each other. That's where the surprises came. Chris discovered that Myrna was much happier and more responsive when he was gentle with her—when he massaged her and stroked her for long, pleasant minutes before initiating intercourse. Myrna discovered that Chris sometimes wished for oral sex but was too inhibited to ask.

They learned and changed. They're much closer now than they were. Chris has strong erections that he sustains in lovemaking for up to half an hour. Myrna is sometimes able to extend orgasm. Their major limiting factor is time—that restaurant still makes its demands.

Men who feel they should automatically know how to stimulate a woman might remember that women don't automatically know how to stimulate them. Neither sex is born with magic fingers nor magic organs. Both have to learn by observation or by being taught. Direct teaching is best.

After each training session, talk about what you experienced and what you learned. Say what you liked about watching each other. Say what surprised you. Say what you didn't like and would do differently next time. *Spend at least five minutes after each session debriefing.* That can be painful, too, but it's crucially important. Talk about your feelings. Use the "Withholds" exercise we describe in the next chapter.

When you know sexual anatomy, when you're regularly doing Kegel exercises, when you've learned well to pleasure yourselves and each other, and when you can easily communicate your sexual feelings, you may be ready to get together for ESO.

In the section on communicating, in the Appendix of this book, we describe more structures for teaching each other pleasure. Look at "Getting to Know You" (p. 198) and "Pleasure Turns" (p. 199). "An Hour of Pleasure" (p. 199) and "Sensory Focus" (p. 200) can also be useful and fun.

IV

GETTING TOGETHER

Talking About Feelings

By now you should know yourself and your partner better than you did before you began reading this book. Simple exercises and physical exploration reach beyond the physical into the emotional. We'd be surprised if you haven't discovered strong feelings about some of what you've learned.

We hope you have. We hope you've talked about them. And we hope talking hasn't deteriorated into argument. It's easy, especially where sex is concerned, to hurt each other's feelings. It's easy to misunderstand. We advise couples we work with to practice a daily communication exercise that helps clear the air. We recommend it equally to you. You may find yourselves resisting it at first, for the usual reason: because it can feel silly. But it's a good basic format for communicating. Many of our client couples tell us that communication exercises soon become second nature to them, part of their normal, day-to-day conversation.

Withholds

The exercise we have in mind is called "Withholds." Withholds are the feelings and resentments about your partner that you are afraid to share for fear of an argument. Withholds are also those overlooked appreciations that you might think your partner already knows. No one tires of hearing expressions of appreciation. Everyone likes approval and honest compliments.

Six months ago you may have told your partner how you enjoy her sense of humor or how you admire his strength, but all of us love to hear those things said much more often. In the beginning, when you were dating, you complimented one another a lot, didn't you? Appreciation binds a relationship together. None of us ever outgrows our need for appreciation, warmly and openly expressed. If partners don't find approval from each other, they may be tempted to look for it elsewhere.

The best way to encourage your partner to continue doing something you want done is to tell him or her how much you enjoy it. Failing to communicate encouragement will make your partner anxious.

To begin the Withholds exercise, say to your partner, in a neutral tone of voice: "(Name), there's something I've withheld from you." Your partner then replies, "Okay. Would you like to tell me?" You say, "Yes." Then share your Withhold. When you are finished, your partner ends the communication cycle by saying "Thank you" and nothing further.

Be sure you use this precise structure. It automatically alerts you to the beginning of the exercise and reminds you both to follow the rules. It announces that a special communication is starting and reminds you to set aside old patterns of reaction that often generate anger and cause arguments. Be sure you announce your Withholds in a neutral, not an emotional, angry, nagging, or sarcastic tone of voice. That way your partner will hear the *content* of your message clearly and won't be distracted by the tone.

Beginning with these opening statements, each partner then spends two or three minutes verbally appreciating the other partner and mentioning any resentments. Or each partner mentions two appreciations and two resentments and then the other mentions two and two. After each appreciation or resentment, the only allowable response is "Thank you." The listening partner agrees to make no other comment until at least thirty minutes after the exercise, and then only with permission. Total time: five minutes a day.

There are at least two good reasons for balancing resentments with appreciations: because then your partner hears your resentments better and because expressions of appreciation between partners are almost always overlooked in favor of criticism. Very few of us are as thoughtful as we ought to be.

You might mention small things:

"Judy, there's something I've withheld from you."

"Okay, would you like to tell me?"

"Yes. I like the way you did your hair today."

"Thank you."

"Judy, there's something I've withheld from you."

"Okay, would you like to tell me?"

"Yes. I really enjoyed it when you fixed my favorite meal last night."

"Thank you."

"Judy, there's something I've withheld from you."

"Okay, would you like to tell me?"

"Yes. When you didn't want to visit my parents, I felt angry and disappointed with you."

"Thank you."

You might bring up major issues: "Bob, there's something I've withheld from you."

"Okay, would you like to tell me?"

"Yes. I felt jealous and excluded when you were talking to that pretty blond lady at the party for so long. When I came over, you seemed to ignore me and continued to talk to her without including me."

"Thank you."

"I know we were going to wait until you got your career settled, but I'm feeling as if I'd like to try for a baby soon."

"Thank you."

The point of Withholds is safe communication. You have feelings you'd like to express, but you keep quiet because you don't want to make your partner mad. By agreeing on a structure for communication that forbids argument, you make it safe. That way you learn more about each other, more honestly. You also build trust. Too many couples we've seen communicate only their resentments. They hardly ever thank or compliment each other.

You can use Withholds more specifically for sexual communication by agreeing sometimes to limit your likes and dislikes to sexual matters. Don't then practice the exercise immediately before, during, or immediately after lovemaking. Choose a more neutral period of time.

For example, a wife might say to her husband:

"Jim, there's something I've withheld from you."

"Okay. Would you like to tell me?"

"Yes—I really appreciated your initiating sex last night. I know you were tired."

"Thank you."

"Jim, there's something else I've withheld from you."

"Okay. Would you like to tell me?"

"Yes. Sometimes, when you're stimulating my clitoris, you lose direct contact with it. I start to come down, then you push harder with your fingers rather than try to locate my clitoris more gently."

"Thank you."

Do the general exercise every day to improve communication with your partner. The sexual exercise should be fitted in among your sessions of lovemaking as part of learning ESO. Use it after you've learned ESO whenever it seems appropriate to make sure you're staying in touch.

Many people resist doing these Withholds at first. They claim, for example, that they have nothing to say. But even people who've known each other for only five minutes can find qualities they appreciate and resent about one another. Couples who've been together for months or years have available a vast stockpile of appreciations and resentments— thousands of past experiences plus all the new feelings that come up each and every day that a couple is together.

Some people resist Withholds by claiming they already communicate well with their partners. But Withholds are different from even exceptional natural communication because they're structured. They require openness and they purposely hold anger and resentment temporarily in abeyance. So there's much value in doing them even for a couple that already communicates well. Please practice them for five minutes a day every day you're together for at least two weeks before you pass judgment on their value for your relationship. The results will almost certainly surprise you.

For several other useful communication exercises, see "Communicating," p. 194.

More About Trust

We said earlier that trust is vital to ESO. We'd like to say more about that now.

ESO requires *both* partners to give their full attention to one of their sexual systems at a time. That double attention greatly increases the pleasure. If you are the passive, receiving partner, you concentrate on your own feelings while the active partner *also* concentrates on your feelings. You give up control to the active partner. That's where the trust comes in—trust that you won't be hurt, trust that your partner will learn what to do to stimulate you in a way that will allow you to let go of your resistances to pleasure.

Only by your teaching, verbal and nonverbal, can your partner learn to stimulate you effectively. *You are the only final authority on your own sexual response.* People often believe that they should know instinctively how to satisfy their partners. But every human being's response to sexual stimulation is different. So no one, man or woman, can know your response in advance. They have to be taught.

That teaching requires trust. If, when you say "That feels uncomfortable. Try a lighter touch," your partner gets mad and says "Oh, the hell with you. If I'm not doing it right, do it yourself. This is stupid," then no one is going to learn. Instead, each of you needs to put your ego aside, say "Thank you," and follow directions.

Sex is a skill. No one is automatically an expert. Each of you is responsible only for understanding your own response. Your partner's response you'll have to learn from the only living expert—your partner. You'll learn more quickly by following the guidelines in this book.

Saying Yes to Sex

One of the most effective ways we know to build trust in a relationship is to make an agreement with your partner always to say yes to sex. There are very few valid reasons for refusing. If lovemaking is inconvenient at the time your partner asks you, you can offer an alternative time. "I'd like to finish what I'm doing right now, but I'd love for us to have sex about an hour after dinner tonight." You *must* keep that agreement. Otherwise your partner will learn not to trust you.

The idea of never denying sex to their partners frightens

some people. They use sex as a weapon and don't want to disarm. But using sex as a weapon creates enormous distrust and resentment in the victim. So the weapon eventually turns back emotional injury to the user. No one wins that war.

Others fear that sex is somehow addictive. Without denial, they think, it will spiral out of control. If denial has been a part of your relationship, your partner is likely to ask to make love more often when denial is set aside. Partly that's a way of testing a newfound agreement. Partly it's a way of establishing a new pattern of lovemaking free of control. Partly it's a response to the novelty of the arrangement.

But sex isn't addictive. To the contrary, the problem for most sexually active couples—even couples skilled at ESO— is finding time for regular sex in the midst of all their other activities.

Sometimes we prescribe an orgasm a day for clients we treat in therapy. That's a healthy goal to have. It ought to be a pleasant prescription, more fun than its predecessor, an apple a day, but our clients complain about the time it takes. After ESO training, that attitude changes. Even a "quickie" finds both partners in enthusiastic agreement.

We should add that we also sometimes find it useful to prescribe, for a few weeks or months, for couples in severe conflict, no sex at all. Because wonderful as it is, routine sex obviously doesn't cure every ill. We prescribe thoughtfulness and other demonstrations of affection—holding hands, hugging, kissing, romantic attention—as substitutes.

Finally, some people fear saying yes because they don't enjoy sex. Once a week, once a month, is more than enough for them. Since sex is a skill, that's a vicious circle. You can't improve—or even maintain what you have—without practice. Neither can your partner.

Agreeing to sex builds trust by freeing each other of rejection. You accept your partner's sexual needs as your responsibility; your partner accepts yours. Women in partic-

Male Stimulating Female

(1) Kneeling
Easy access to genitals with both hands. Good for
intimate eye contact and expressions of love. Easy
transition to kneeling-over position.

ular learn the pleasure of asking for lovemaking when they want it. That's something many women don't trust their partners enough to do.

Men who believe they're sexual failures if they don't anticipate all their partner's needs find mutual sexual responsibility frees them from that pressure. When they grow beyond feeling threatened, they discover that it's flattering to be asked.

Connecting

Before you begin touching or stimulating each other, it's important to connect mentally. One way to do that is to talk about pleasant times and experiences, past or imagined. Keep your talk light and positive. It's the wrong time to bring up balancing your checkbook or handling your mother-in-law.

Silent eye contact can help you connect. Sitting or lying down, facing each other, look at one of your partner's eyes or at the center forehead. Resist any tendency to talk or giggle. Allow yourself to be comfortable and relaxed with yourself and your partner. Think peaceful, positive thoughts. Imagine being absorbed by your partner's eyes.

Dancing Hands is another useful exercise. Sitting facing one another, making solid eye contact, hold your hands at chest level with palms toward your partner while your partner does the same. Your palms should almost—but not quite—touch. One of you leads by moving your hands up, down, sideways, and around at varying speed. The other follows intuitively. After about two minutes, leader becomes follower for two minutes. Continue to alternate silently until you feel connected.

Sexual Exploration

Sexual Exploration is an exercise in teaching each other where you're sensitive to pleasure. It's best done at home, in bed, when you've both bathed and have a space of private time together.

You'll take turns. Decide who's first. Get a hand mirror. Refer to the drawings of the male and female genitals. See illustrations number 1 and 7 for body positions.

First take turns pointing out and naming all the pelvic and genital structures. Find the glans penis, the glans clitoris, and so on.

Then apply a lubricant and explore your partner's genitals, using strokes of different lengths and pressures. Your partner should experience each stroke and rate it on a scale of −10 to +10, the minus numbers indicating discomfort, the plus numbers indicating comfort and pleasure.

Spend a minimum of ten minutes per person in this exploration and go over each of the genital structures in turn. The man should insert a finger into the woman's vagina to explore the sensations in different areas. A way to describe the areas is by reference to the hours on a clock face: twelve o'clock, upward toward the navel; one o'clock, moving right; three o'clock, halfway down; and so on. The woman should try squeezing the penis in both its soft and its hard states until the man indicates discomfort, so she can learn how much pressure the penis can take. Both partners should explore, in the course of several sessions, until they learn their partner's anatomy and unique areas of sensitivity well.

Afterward, spend a few minutes discussing what you were thinking and feeling and what you learned. Please

Female Stimulating Male

(2) **Between Legs, Head on Thigh**
   Right hand stimulates penis; left hand stimulates penis/external prostate. Good for adding oral stimulation.

practice Sexual Exploration at least once even if you think
you have done something similar or if it seems elementary.
Everyone, including sexually experienced couples who have
been together for a long time, can benefit from practicing this
exercise once in a while. Physical responses change. So do
psychological needs. It's a way of staying in touch.

Foreplay

Foreplay—petting—is as necessary a preliminary to ESO
as it is to ordinary lovemaking. It follows naturally from
bathing together and drying each other off. When you're
naked together, when you've lain down together, begin by
touching each other for pleasure. Explore each other's body.
Tease. Giggle. Have fun!

Women especially tend to resent immediate genital stimulation. They feel used. Don't emphasize the genitals at first.
Kiss and caress. Enjoy the warmth of skin, the weight and
texture of muscle and flesh. The skin is the body's largest
sense organ. Human beings need to be touched.

Directing your attention outward or inward is a skill you
will use for ESO. You can improve it during foreplay. When
you touch your partner to *give* pleasure, you're directing
your attention outward. It's possible then to shift that attention and direct it inward—to notice how touching your
partner feels to *you*. Then a sense of your partner's body—
the sexiness of her curves, of his muscles—flows back
through your fingertips.

We're not speaking poetically. Directing your attention is
mental, but it's real. We all do it. If you're watching a
favorite show, concentrating on reading the newspaper, or

daydreaming, you may not hear what someone in the room says. Your attention is elsewhere. Couples can use this skill of directing attention for pleasure.

You can easily shift your attention back and forth from outward to inward. Pleasure builds if you do. In ESO training you'll use this skill to help clear away distractions and work through resistance. Foreplay is a good time to practice.

There's another kind of shifting attention that gives pleasure. It happens when you touch your partner for pleasure and your partner responds to that touch with increased arousal. Then you in turn are aroused by your partner's response. When you take turns pleasuring each other to ESO, you'll find that your partner's arousal stimulates your own.

Massage

Massage can be a part of foreplay, but it's optional. You might casually spend several minutes massaging your partner's face, hands, feet, back. You might offer a full-body massage. Reach an agreement before you begin on longer massages:

"For the next ten minutes I'd like to give you a massage."

"Okay."

That relieves the receiver of guilt. Your partner knows what to expect and can relax and enjoy the experience. If you pay some attention to the pleasure coming back to you from massaging, you'll enjoy the experience too.

Several good books have been published about massage. You may want to refer to the bibliography at the end of this book to locate one to learn the details of technique.

Sensory Focus

Sensory Focus is an excellent way to move from day-to-day thoughts and worries into sensuality. It slows down the unromantic rush of hopping into bed and diving for the genitals. Especially if you are concerned about your or your partner's sexual functioning, you should practice this graduated set of exercises frequently. We describe Sensory Focus in full detail in the appendix on p. 200.

Mutual Stimulation

With this exercise you can improve sexual communication and increase trust while you build mutual sexual arousal.

Both partners lie on their sides, resting on their elbows, facing each other's genitals (see illustration number 5 for position). The woman's left hand stimulates the shaft and glans of the penis. Her right hand is free to stimulate the scrotum and external prostate spot. The man stimulates the clitoris with his left hand and the vagina with his right. Both partners should use lubrication.

Stimulate each other simultaneously for at least thirty minutes. While you're doing so, talk to each other about your feelings and reactions. Tell your partner what feels good, what doesn't, what you'd like done differently.

If one of you becomes bored or loses excitement, say so. Your partner can give you suggestions for redirecting your attention to increasing pleasure and can alter the stimulation you're getting.

Note that each partner is free to provide oral stimulation. Keep it brief for now; oral stimulation limits talk.

Do this exercise at least three times a week for at least one week. You'll find it useful to repeat from time to time as a way of staying in touch.

Taking Turns

In this step-by-step progression toward ESO another preliminary is to agree on who will first be cause and who will first be effect: who will give pleasure first and who will receive.

Taking turns pleasuring is vital to achieving ESO. It allows the partner being pleasured to let go of outward attention and concentrate on inward feelings. The pleasured partner needs to be completely free of concern about what to do next, what comes next, how the other person feels—actively experiencing, but allowing the partner to take charge. That's why trust is crucial to success.

We advise couples learning ESO to begin with the man pleasuring and the woman being pleasured. If a man has orgasm with ejaculation, he's not as likely to give his partner his full attention afterward. A woman is potentially capable of many orgasms. If, taking her pleasure first, she has an orgasm, that only adds to the experience; it doesn't end it. A woman needs to feel cared for. She may not trust her partner to give her the pleasure she requires. Once her partner has pleasured her to orgasm she will trust him more and thus more easily let go of resistance. It's a wise man who takes care of his partner first. Her enthusiasm to stimulate him when his turn comes will be his delightful reward.

Later, when you've learned ESO, you can vary the sequence. While you're learning, the rule is women first. It works better that way.

Are You Ready for ESO?

You're ready to begin practicing to experience ESO when:

(1) you and your partner both agree that you understand each other's anatomy.

(2) men: you can stimulate yourself to a reliable erection within five minutes and peak yourself—stopping just short of ejaculation—at least six times in a thirty-minute period.

(3) women: you can have orgasm reliably with self-stimulation, using only your hands, without a vibrator.

(4) men: you can reliably stimulate your partner to an orgasm within twenty minutes, using your hands, your mouth, or both.

(5) women: you can stimulate your partner with your hands, your mouth, or both to a reliable erection within five minutes and can peak him, stopping just short of ejaculation, at least six times in a thirty-minute period.

(6) you can both comfortably express and hear your sexual appreciations and resentments.

If you have difficulty with number one, review the anatomy descriptions in this book with your partner and then review your partner's anatomy, using the Sexual Exploration exercise (p. 72).

If you have difficulty with numbers two or three, review the discussion of self-stimulation in this book and keep practicing.

If you have difficulty with numbers four or five, turn to Chapter III, "Developing Skills," to the section called "Communicating Sexually" (p. 60). Review and practice Sensory Focus Steps III and IV. Include in your review the exercise Taking Charge in the appendix on p. 200.

If you have difficulty with number six, review and continue to practice the exercises in this chapter. Do Withholds faithfully every day.

If you continue to have difficulty, read "Solving Problems," the appendix at the end of this book, which begins on p. 169. If you fit any of those problem categories, follow the advice we give there.

After you've solved any difficulties, proceed to the next chapter. You're ready to begin practicing to experience ESO!

V

ESO: GIVING A WOMAN PLEASURE

Preparations

This chapter will tell you, the man, how to stimulate your female partner to ESO.* "You" here will mean the active, stimulating partner. Both partners should read this chapter carefully before going on. Much that we'll have to say applies equally to men and women.

After a time of pleasant foreplay, the woman finds a comfortable position lying on her back. She props her head on a pillow if she likes. She separates her legs. She can flex them, knees raised, or extend them. Comfort with access is the key.

You may kneel, sit cross-legged, lie on your stomach, lie beside your partner or between her legs, arranging yourself

*These directions apply equally to homosexual couples where female stimulates female.

81

so that you can see and easily touch her genitals. You may locate yourself on her left side so that your right hand has access to her clitoris and your left hand to her vagina. Or you may prefer to be on her right so that you can use your right hand for vaginal stimulation. Be comfortable. Use your hands as they work best for you.

Now carefully apply lubricant—warming it first in your hand—to your partner's entire genital area: major labia, minor labia, the clitoris and its structures, the opening of the vagina, a little way into the vagina itself, and down along the perineum. The external anal area responds pleasurably to stimulation. If your partner likes stimulation there, lubricate the anal area too.

Too much lubricant is better than too little. Be generous. Even though it's nonabsorbent, some of it will melt away or be absorbed by the skin. Remember that a woman's genital lubrication comes from the inner walls of her vagina. The clitoris produces no natural lubricant of its own.

Begin now lightly stimulating the external genitals—the pubic hair, the major labia. Lightly brushing the pubic hair, gently pulling it, creates arousal, because all the structures in the area are connected. What you're doing is a localized version of foreplay, gradually approaching the sensitive areas enclosed within the major and minor labia. Just as you did in foreplay, you're following the principle of general stimulation before localized stimulation. When women plea-sure themselves, they usually do the same thing, caressing the overall genital area before concentrating on the clitoris.

In a sense, you're teasing. Teasing creates arousal. You circle the clitoris, slowly closing in. Press lightly with the palm of your hand or several fingers together on the major labia and the pubic hair. Then, over a period of a minute or two, gradually make teasing circles closer to the clitoris. Brush the clitoris sometimes as your hand circles.

Stroking the Clitoris

When you approach the clitoris itself, touch it only lightly at first. All the nerve endings found in the glans penis are concentrated into the clitoris's small area. It's extremely sensitive.

Every woman's preference for clitoral stimulation is unique. Some women like a very light touch. Some prefer the clitoral shaft stroked rather than the glans. Others don't want the clitoris touched directly at all. Sometimes the clitoris is more sensitive on the right side, sometimes on the left. You need to get to know your partner's clitoris well. You and your partner's clitoris need to become intimate friends.

You began that friendship with sexual communication training in Chapter III. You saw the clitoris change shape, color, and position with sexual arousal. Now you need to extend your knowledge by giving your partner's clitoris your close, full attention. Your goal at this point is to stimulate your partner to orgasm with your hand. (You may already have found successful ways to do that. Read this section through anyway to learn about their application to ESO.)

No single stroke will work reliably for all women. You'll have to proceed by trial and error. Your partner showed you what felt good to her during sexual communication training. Apply that information now.

Many women complain that their men don't experiment enough with different kinds of strokes. Or that the experimenting happens too fast, the man moving from one stroke to another before the woman has had time to relax with it and see how it feels.

To find a stroke that your partner likes, try different areas of the clitoris and different pressures on the clitoris. Change strokes only gradually. Watch your partner's response. If her genitals are becoming more engorged, you're doing fine. The best way to approach the clitoris is with thumb and forefinger. Your thumb at the top of the clitoris—toward the stomach—anchors it. Your forefinger strokes it lower down. (See illustration number 3.) You stroke one side for a while, the top, the other side. The motion can be up and down or circling, and the thumb can rock. Or roll the clitoris lightly between forefinger and thumb. (See illustration number 1.) Try these variations; make up others as you go.

Your basic stroke should be slow and steady, about one cycle per second.

Women clients often tell us that their partners aren't consistent with stimulation. Find a consistent pattern and keep it up for several minutes at a time without change, except the changes we mention below.

Watch your partner's reaction. If a stroke is working, it arouses her. You see the arousal. Her genital area swells, adding fullness to the major and minor labia. Her clitoris enlarges and moves downward and inward. The clitoral glans engorges much as the glans of your penis does with erection. The vaginal area and the clitoris darken from the added flow of blood.

Your partner can guide you by making sounds. If what you're doing feels right, she can moan, hum, sigh with pleasure. Vocalizing during lovemaking is arousing in itself. It also lets you know that arousal is happening. Talking at this point is distracting; that's why nonverbal vocalizing is a valuable skill to learn.

Your partner will also guide you by moving her pelvis toward your hand or away. If your stroking is arousing her, if she is climbing toward orgasm, she will press her genitals into your hand because she is reaching for more stimulation. If the stimulation is ineffective or uncomfortable, or if she is resisting, she'll move her genitals away. These movements are subtle. They may amount to shifts of only a quarter of an inch or so, against your hand or away.

Look as well for larger signs of arousal, especially muscle tension. Pelvic muscle tension and general body muscle tension are signs of sexual arousal. So are sighs, panting, jerky movements, sweating, curling of the toes and feet.

If your partner moves away even slightly from your hand, you need to back off. That doesn't mean lifting your hand completely away. It means letting up a little on pressure, slightly slowing your stroke or moving your fingers to a slightly different area of her clitoris. The clitoris is small. Your changes in response to your partner's signals need to be small too.

It helps to be able to see your partner's genitals. As you're learning ESO it also helps from time to time to close your eyes and sense what the structures you're stimulating feel like. That way, your hands learn as well as your eyes.

Building Arousal

A teasing cycle builds arousal. When you've found a basic stroke that your partner likes, use it for about ten strokes and then relax to a resting stroke—lighter or slower or not so directly applied to the clitoris—for a stroke or two. That increases sexual tension. Your partner will signal her arousal by moving her genitals toward your hand, asking for the stimulating stroke again. Ten stimulating (climbing) strokes to one or two resting strokes is a good pattern to follow. It's not the only pattern. Six to one may be better for your partner, or three to one, or fifteen to one. Experiment and see.

You can build to extremely high levels of arousal with only your thumb and forefinger. For a variation, add the middle finger, so you have three fingers cradling the clitoris. (See illustration number 3 inset.) The thumb continues to anchor the clitoris from above; the forefinger and the middle finger

Male Stimulating Female

(3) Lying on Elbow
   Comfortable. Easy access to clitoris and vagina with hands and mouth. Left hand demonstrates basic clitoral stimulation stroke with thumb and forefinger grasping clitoris. Thumb anchors clitoral base; forefinger strokes glans.

   Inset shows three-fingered variation of clitoral stroke. Thumb anchors base; forefinger and middle finger cradle clitoris and stroke sides.

then stroke the sides of the clitoris and its base. This is an excellent clitoral control stroke. The point is to find the best way to build arousal to higher and higher levels, always backing off when the climbing stops.

At any time during this initial stimulation you can insert one or two fingers of your other hand into your partner's vagina. That hand won't be especially active yet, although you may add to your partner's arousal by sweeping a finger around her vagina while you stroke her clitoris. Your forefinger or middle finger at least needs to be comfortably inserted into your partner's vagina by the time she begins orgasm.

Resistances

While you're stroking her clitoris, what's your partner doing? (Men: this discussion will apply equally to you when you're being stimulated. Read it carefully.)

She's actively aware. She's totally focused on her own experience. That experience is a combination of feeling and thinking. The more that she can pay attention to feeling, the more she will feel. But part of the time your partner will be thinking, because thinking is a habit. Some of her thinking—especially her doubts, questions, and worries—will get in the way of arousal. That's resistance and it blocks feelings. Your partner needs to learn to identify that kind of thinking quickly. When it's your turn, so will you.

A list of the things people tell themselves to deny themselves pleasure would be longer than this book. Ironically, everyone resists pleasure. Your partner struggles with resistances while you pleasure her. You will struggle with them when your partner pleasures you. Even men and women thoroughly experienced in ESO encounter resistances. Experience teaches them how to let go of resistances more quickly whenever they come up during sexual stimulation.

Your partner is resisting when she
(1) subtly pulls away from you;
(2) shows less engorgement or lubrication;
(3) opens her eyes and looks bored.

Many resistances come in the form of intrusive thoughts. Sometimes such thoughts are continuous. At other times they occur intermittently—for a few seconds, perhaps, several times a minute. Here are a few common intrusive thoughts:

He's getting tired.
That's enough.
I don't deserve any more.
I'm afraid.
I feel like I'm going to burst.
I wonder what that sound was?
I wonder if the kids/parents/neighbors can hear?
This is wrong.
I want a cigarette/a cup of coffee.
I want to go to the bathroom.
I wonder if I smell?
I'm not attractive enough.
Tomorrow I've got to . . .
Yesterday I should have . . .
I don't think I can do this.
I don't have time for this.
I should be:
   checking the kids
   cleaning the house
   getting ready for work tomorrow.
He has time for me only when he wants sex.
He's just using me.
He/She doesn't care how I feel.
This is boring.

Resistances are ways we limit ourselves. But resistances are normal. They're the necessary friction of love. In the context of sexual pleasure they're not wrong or bad and they're no one's fault. They're simply barriers that have to be worked through, every single time they arise.

Don't blame each other for resistances. If you do, you won't trust each other. If you don't trust each other, you can't fully let go to pleasure.

For a thorough discussion of resistances, see Chapter VIII, "Overcoming Resistances," p. 141.

Controlling Thought

There are two basic ways to control the thoughts that make up resistances. Your partner needs to apply both of them while you're stimulating her.

One way is to change the thought. The technical term for deliberately changing thoughts is "cognitive restructuring." When a distracting thought pops into your partner's head, she needs to replace it with a positive thought: "This feels good. I'm safe. I'll let that thought go." Cognitive restructuring isn't mumbo jumbo. It's a commonplace of psychology and it works.

A variation of cognitive restructuring is replacing a distracting thought with a neutral thought. That's the basic technique of meditation systems that teach the use of mantras—of neutral, sometimes nonsense words. The neutral thought can be a relaxation phrase—"I'm calm"—or a repeated number, or a sound like the classic mantra "Om." The neutral thought isn't sexually arousing, but it displaces the distracting thought and allows your partner to pay attention again to sensation.

That's the other basic way to control thoughts: by redirecting attention *inward* to sensation and allowing the physical experience to take over again. Your job is to make sure the sensation is steadily available when your partner needs it.

Many men, when they sense their partners leveling off or coming down from arousal, try to crash through the resistance by speeding up their stroke or by pressing harder. It's usually much better to let your partner work through her resistance herself. If you supply steady, rhythmic, reliable, pleasurable stimulation, she'll have the sensation she needs to find her way.

When you feel your partner resisting, back off slightly. The slight change should help her refocus her attention on the sensation you're providing.

When You're Stuck

After a while, if your partner is still coming down, try backing off a little more. If the blockage continues—if your partner continues to lose arousal—you may then want to try the opposite approach, increasing stimulation to help her push through. Do it subtly. You certainly don't want to create pain. You don't want your partner to feel that you're demanding she go on. Pay attention to the effect you're causing. If increasing stimulation makes your partner even more resistant, then back off once more.

Many couples get stuck at this point. It's a tricky, difficult moment, loaded with frustration. Couples get stuck and eventually give up. The man's tired, the woman's tired, they're angry with each other. He silently accuses her of resisting him. She silently accuses him of trying to force her to respond. Both people forget the point, which is pleasure. No one benefits.

If your partner is obviously coming down from arousal in a major way—if the resistance has completely taken over and she can't find her way through—you both should stop what you're doing and talk about what's happening.

Be affectionate with each other—be loving. Don't make accusations. You've hit a snag. Everybody does. Discuss it. Resistance is normal. It's part of the process. If it weren't, we'd all have sex all the time and forget to eat. You can even have fun with resistance by making overcoming it a game.

See what you can find out about what you were doing and what your partner was feeling. Then begin again if your partner feels more comfortable. Or switch roles and move on. Since you're working on ESO at least three times a week, neither of you ever needs to feel left out for long. You can always complete lovemaking in your usual way. ESO isn't exclusive. It adds range and depth to what you already have.

Using Kegel Exercises

Another way your partner can overcome resistance is to contract her P.C. muscles deliberately by doing Kegel exercises while you are stimulating her. Resistance often shows up as muscle tension—tightening muscles, deliberately or unconsciously—which, when prolonged, works against arousal. But then relaxing those same muscles after tension usually leads to an increase in arousal. Many people, to build arousal, find themselves alternately tensing and relaxing their muscles—the P.C. muscles at least, and often their entire bodies.

Kegel exercises add an important third step to this process because they're a three-part exercise. The first step is tension, the second is release, and the third is pushing out—bearing down. Your partner can work through resistance by doing all three steps while you're stroking her. Not only does this help to increase arousal directly, it also focuses your partner's attention on muscular sensations rather than negative thoughts.

Do what it takes to overcome resistance, remembering the cautions we've mentioned. Even a light slap on the clitoris or the opening of the vagina can sometimes help startle resistance away. It shouldn't be hard enough to cause resentment or pain. It's another variation to experiment with.

Breakthrough Breathing

People frequently block orgasm by holding their breath. Breath holding usually follows from muscle tensing. A woman pushes out with her P.C. muscles to build arousal. When she pushes out and bears down, she holds her breath. Up to a point, holding her breath increases arousal, but some women hold their breath for half a minute or more.

If your partner has the habit of holding her breath when she's tensing her body or clamping her P.C. muscles to reach for arousal (you can tell if she does by noticing her breathing while you're stroking her), she should practice breathing more deliberately. We normally breathe about twelve times a minute. Climbing in sexual arousal, your partner should still breathe at least six times a minute. The best way to pay attention to breathing is to experience it. Your partner should *feel* taking in a breath—air moving into her nose and mouth and filling her lungs—and then exhaling it down toward her genitals. You can help by reminding her to breathe when you notice she's holding her breath.

Breathing to a counting rhythm is another very useful technique your partner can use for breakthrough breathing. She counts silently to six (or four, or ten—whatever is comfortable), about one count per second, as she breathes in and again as she breathes out: IN two, three, four, five, six, OUT two, three, four, five, six, IN . . .

Paralleling her change in breathing, your partner should practice keeping the rest of her body relaxed when she tenses her pelvic muscles. That puts the muscle tension in her genitals, where it's useful, and makes breathing easier.

Doing Kegel exercises while counting breaths teaches this technique. We can't stress too much the importance of Kegel exercises. The more of these exercises you and your partner do and the more regularly you do them, the better for sex. The bigger and stronger the P.C. muscle gets, the more feeling you'll have. Combining the two powerful techniques of breakthrough breathing and Kegel exercises will add a turbocharge to your sexual experience.

Switching to the Vagina

Eventually—building arousal, working through resistances, climbing and leveling and climbing—your partner will begin the regular one-second contractions of regular orgasm. At that point *switch your attention to her vagina*. She may want you to continue clitoral stroking during these first contractions. If so, do, but you'll probably need to lighten up. Any but the lightest stimulation will probably be uncomfortable. You may need now to lift your hand entirely away from the clitoris.

Continue vaginal stimulation through these first orgasmic contractions and after they taper off. You can move your fingers in and out of your partner's vagina in a motion imitating the thrusting of your penis, or sweep them around the vaginal barrel. But the most effective stimulation is rhythmic stroking with one or two fingers of the area called the G spot.

An anatomy refresher: the G spot is the area about one and a half inches inside the vagina just behind the pubic bone in the center and front of the vagina. It's one to two fingers wide, rubber- or sponge-like, firmer than the rest of the vaginal wall. It gets firmer still when it's stimulated, which makes it easier to find. Remember, some women identify a general area rather than a particular spot. That's the area to stimulate.

By stimulating your partner's vagina when her orgasm begins, you'll cause a sharp increase even then in her arousal. If you directly stimulate the G spot much before orgasm, your partner may find it uncomfortable. But once orgasm begins, G spot stimulation is arousing rather than uncomfortable. The G spot can then take hard pressure, while the clitoris, which was stimulated before by regular stroking, now responds to more than the very lightest touch with something like pain. You've probably noticed a similar sensation. Most men find touching the glans penis painful immediately after ejaculation. So pay attention to your partner's vagina rather than to her clitoris at this volatile time.

Extended Sexual Orgasm

When you switch attention to your partner's vagina while she's having orgasmic contractions, you continue to supply her with a high level of stimulation. Whether you're moving your fingers in and out of her vagina or stroking her G spot with your fore- or middle finger, you should continue the regular, once-per-second rhythm you established when you stroked her clitoris earlier. Continue building on that ten-to-one—or six-to-one, whatever worked best—cycle, increasing and decreasing pressure.

This internal stimulation creates a deeper kind of contraction than the superficial (outer one-third) vaginal muscle contractions of single orgasm. The deeper contractions involve the deep pelvic musculature, including the big muscles of the uterus. These deeper contractions are longer and more pleasurable. They represent the physical basis for female extended sexual orgasm: ESO. The contractions in this first phase of ESO are variable in length, lasting from one to ten seconds each.

The vagina responds to single orgasm by tenting—by enlarging at the back and lifting up into the body. To a finger inserted into the vagina, that response feels like a loosening and a pulling away. (See the illustration "Female Anatomy.")

With the beginning of ESO your partner's vagina will respond to your stimulating finger by *pushing out*, as if the uterus were pushing toward the opening of the vagina and closing the vaginal space. (See inset of "Female Anatomy" illustration, "Push-out Contractions.")

When you feel that pushing, your partner is beginning to have a deep pelvic orgasmic contraction that may herald the beginning of ESO.

When you feel your partner's vagina drawing back—pulling away—then she's leveling and you should lighten the pressure you're applying inside the vagina and slow your stroke. Soon your partner will begin to want more stimulation again. You add pressure and speed up your stroke and she begins to push out against your fingers again. That means you're supplying the right amount of stimulation. You can continue at that level. Or you can increase the pressure and rate to bring on more climbing. Higher arousal may eventually lead to resistance, and you will feel your partner's vagina again withdrawing, signaling you to lighten and slow your stroke.

When she starts to level—when there's a pause in her climbing—switch your attention away from the vagina and return your attention to stimulating the clitoris.

Stimulating the clitoris at this point usually results in one or more squeeze contractions. Those contractions signal that you should once again switch your attention to the inner trigger area of the vagina. Look for a push-out contraction then—that will mean your partner is experiencing her most rapid form of climbing. You should continue the kind of stimulation that best works to produce continuous waves of push-out contractions.

Two factors determine the intensity and frequency of your partner's push-outs: the speed, pressure, and location of your stimulating inner finger or fingers; and your partner's skill at letting go of her resistances to climbing continuously toward more pleasure.

When your partner's climbing stops—when her push-outs cease—once again immediately shift your attention from the G spot and focus more on the clitoris. Within a few seconds you should notice contractions, either squeeze or push-out. That's your signal to redirect your stimulation to the vaginal trigger area again. If your pattern of rhythmic stimulation is correct, the periods of time between contractions, squeeze or push-out, will be very brief—approximately one to five seconds. Your partner's experience of continuous contractions of either kind will be longer—in the range of ten to thirty seconds.

As you continue this pattern for fifteen minutes or more you will find that the brief resting—leveling—periods occur less and less frequently and your partner has contractions more and more of the time. When the leveling or resting periods disappear and her contractions are all deep push-outs, she has entered Phase II ESO.

During the ESO training process *you* will be more in control of the stimulation than your partner. She will have some control of the pushing out—the contractions—and the withdrawing, just as she had some control of moving toward your hand or away when you were stroking her clitoris earlier.

But much more than before, she will be lost in feeling and will be doing very little thinking. She'll be reacting rather than controlling. You'll be in charge of supplying the right stimulation. You need to feel in command. As you learn what you're doing you will. As long as you don't do anything to cause pain, your partner will let you—and should let you—control. When the stimulation is right, she won't move toward you or away. She'll stay where she is and enjoy what she's feeling.

One of our clients, a young woman named Roberta, beautifully articulated the experience of breaking over into ESO. She commented pointedly at the same time on the subtleties of resistance.

"I was amazed at what happened," she told us about her first ESO experience with her boyfriend, Albert. "Instead of *trying* to make myself have orgasm, or being annoyed with Albert for not stimulating me right, I just kind of blanked out for a moment—and I started to have orgasm instantly. Then, instead of tightening up after a few seconds, as I used to do just by habit, I remembered to *breathe* and let my mind blank out again. And I kept on having orgasm! I kept breathing and letting my body do what it wanted to.

"It felt so good," Roberta finished with a grin, "I thought to myself that I never wanted it to stop. Then I got scared. Then, instantly, it *did* stop!" We're glad to say it started again for Roberta as she gained more experience at letting go.

Communication can continue during ESO just as it did before—with body movements, with your careful reading of your partner's responses, with vocalizing. Your partner's body movements and vocalizing are likely to be much more obvious now, because she's experiencing much higher levels of arousal. Moaning, jerky motions of her arms and legs, tossing her head, curling her toes and feet, panting, all are signs you should expect to see in the climbing stages as ESO continues. *The main sign that should guide your stimulation is the vagina pushing outward against your fingers in contraction.*

During *leveling* periods of ESO, your partner will usually be more quiet, her body stiller and her pelvic contractions of the squeeze type.

The graph "Female Orgasmic Responses" shows the differences in arousal and response through time of single orgasm, multiple orgasm, and ESO (Stage I, Stage II, Stage III).

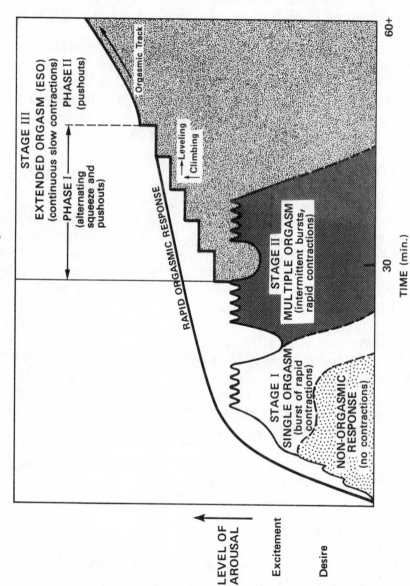

FEMALE ORGASMIC RESPONSES
Three Stages

In single, brief orgasm (Stage I), arousal increases with stimulation through an excitement phase to an orgasm of one-second contractions lasting from four to twelve seconds. Contractions are the superficial, vaginal-"clenching" type. Then arousal declines steadily down to baseline. This is orgasm as Masters and Johnson describe it in *Human Sexual Response.*

Multiple brief orgasm (Stage II) is identical to single brief orgasm except that arousal doesn't immediately decline to baseline. Instead it dips below the orgasmic level to high excitement level. Then, with continuing or renewed stimulation, it returns briefly to the prior orgasmic level with a rapid burst of superficial contractions like those of single orgasm. This process may repeat several times. Eventually arousal returns to baseline.

ESO (Stage III) follows a different development. It passes through the same first phases as Stage I orgasm: excitement and a burst of rapid contractions. Or it can begin after several Stage II multiple-orgasmic responses. But instead of dropping back to the high-excitement level, it continues upward from the orgasmic level to even higher levels of arousal— climbing, leveling, and climbing.

This first phase of ESO is characterized by alternating slow contractions of the superficial vaginal muscles (squeeze contractions) and the deep pelvic muscles (push-out contractions). Both the squeeze and push-out contractions vary in length from one up to thirty seconds. Their intensity also varies depending on your stimulation and your partner's resistance. Contractions during ESO are slower and longer than during Stage I and Stage II orgasm.

The duration and intensity of the deep pelvic contractions depend primarily on the amount of stimulation. You control the duration of a contraction when you stimulate your partner in the climbing process we described. You slow the contractions by decreasing vaginal and clitoral stroking. Your partner will climb to a higher level of arousal during push-out contractions. Then she'll resist and level, her vagina withdrawing from your finger and clenching—squeezing—around it instead. During leveling, she will experience squeeze contractions. Then you increase stimulation and she climbs again and experiences push-out contractions.

Generally, stimulating the clitoris encourages superficial squeeze contractions; stimulating the inner trigger area encourages deep push-out contractions. A combination of alternating and simultaneous stimulation of the clitoris and the inner trigger area is the basic method of the first phase of ESO. We also call this phase the staircase phase because of the way it looks on a graph.

The first phase of ESO may last fifteen minutes or more. When a woman finally lets go of all resistances, she enters the second phase of ESO, the continuous-climbing phase. This second phase of ESO is characterized by smooth, long waves of deep push-out contractions. You create it by stimulating both the clitoris and the vagina at the same time.

To your partner this phase feels timeless. She feels as if she is on an orgasmic track of continuous and smoothly rising pleasure. Like a meditative state, the feeling is of an altered state of consciousness—floating without effort. In the first phase of ESO, the staircase phase, your partner pushes mentally and constantly reaches for more pleasure. In the continuously climbing phase she has no sensation of effort. This experience can last from several minutes to an hour or more.

Some women are able to experience both Phase I and Phase II ESO with clitoral stimulation alone. They can sustain push-out contractions with only clitoral stimulation. Vaginal stimulation still usually adds to the intensity of their experience.

We have preliminary data from electrical brain recordings that show characteristic changes in brain waves occuring during ESO. The brain-wave pattern appears to be different from other states of arousal and other stages of orgasm. We find a possible shift in activity between the left and right hemispheres of the brain, which become more synchronized with each other. These changes are similar to those seen in states of deep meditation.

One of our clients, Natali, calls the experience of second-phase ESO "being nailed." "At a certain point," she told us, "I finally gave up and let go completely. It's as if André had me nailed to the spot and I couldn't move a single muscle. I didn't want to. I wanted to stay there forever." Another client compared the sensation to "floating in space." A third found "no questions, only answers. Problems that had been bothering me for a long time suddenly seemed clear."

After your partner has enjoyed a few minutes of second-phase ESO, she may need less stimulation to maintain the continuous climb. The orgasmic process becomes more self-sustaining. Light stimulation of the vagina and clitoris or of either area alone is usually sufficient then. Orgasmic contractions may even continue for thirty seconds or more with no stimulation at all.

Women trained in ESO report experiencing a level of arousal with extended orgasm different from the arousal of single or multiple brief orgasm. Each orgasm in a series of multiple orgasms, they say, feels much the same as the last one. But ESO feels more and more intense as the stimulation continues. Arousal keeps on increasing during ESO. The vagina feels as if it is taking over. But remember, heart rate and blood pressure actually go down. You won't explode.

The graph on p. 98 shows that continuing increase. We've left it open-ended because we have not yet seen any limit to the level of orgasmic arousal possible—except the obvious limits of a couple's time and energy. Sooner or later one or both of you will get tired or decide you've had enough for now. You'll choose then to come down.

Before then, finish your partner by taking her up to an extra-high peak of orgasmic arousal, a true climax.

Women trained in ESO tell us that they continue to feel occasional deep contractions for up to twenty-four hours after extended orgasmic experience. Which is to say, they continue to be aroused above the baseline state and even feel occasional subtle orgasmic contractions as they go about their day-to-day lives. That's why they may begin orgasm almost immediately upon penetration during intercourse. This is called the Rapid Orgasmic Response. It catapults a woman right back into ESO again. (See graph on p. 98.)

We should add that women who regularly experience ESO function better than ever, whatever their work. And they're healthier, less irritable, more relaxed, and much happier.

VI

ESO: GIVING A MAN
PLEASURE

THIS CHAPTER will tell you, the woman, how to stimulate
your male partner to ESO.* "You" here will mean the
active, stimulating partner. As before, both partners should
read this chapter carefully.

You've enjoyed a time of ESO. Now it's the man's turn.
You may want to proceed immediately to changing places
and switching roles. Or you may want to take a break—for
refreshments, to use the toilet, or simply to rest.

There's no law that says both partners have to experience
ESO every time either one of them does. It's usually advis-
able. In the long run the books of sexual attention need to be
balanced. Otherwise one or the other partner will feel cheat-
ed. Certainly, in training for ESO, you and your partner
should pleasure each other for more or less equivalent periods of time.

*These directions apply equally to homosexual couples where male stimulates male.

Accepting Pleasure

Many men resist being pleasured. They're used to *taking* pleasure. If they're loving men, they're used to giving pleasure. They need to learn to accept lying back and relaxing and letting someone pleasure them. A man's goal at this point is to be totally passive, like a sponge, to see how much pleasure he can absorb. Men need to learn that sex doesn't always have to be a performance (so do you, if you're used to thinking of your partner as a performer).

Rodney was a client of ours who had difficulty accepting pleasure. He was forty-seven when we first saw him. His wife, June, was thirty. The age difference sometimes bothered Rodney, but he was more subtly troubled by the difference in his and June's body sizes. June was slightly larger than he, taller and heavier. The size difference intimidated him.

The problem didn't show up at first as Rodney progressed from early ejaculation to sustaining twenty- and thirty-minute erections and June progressed to beginning ESO. Then the time came for Rodney to allow June to stimulate him manually and orally. He balked. He felt dominated. He was happy to stimulate June. He was happy with intercourse. But he could only accept manual and oral stimulation from June for two or three minutes at a time before he became too uncomfortable, too anxious, to continue.

It wasn't an enormous problem to solve. Rodney concentrated on relaxing through his resistance. We suggested that June use one of the lower-profile positions we'll be telling you about, so that she didn't seem to tower over her husband as he lay on his back. She reassured him verbally that she found his body attractive. Rodney eventually learned to accept pleasure from June. They're doing very well.

Men who feel uncomfortable lying back and taking should remember that they've just given their partners an intense time of pleasure. They've done their duty. It's fair and right that they should have pleasure in return.

Men: your partner deserves the same experience of giving you intense pleasure as you had giving pleasure to her. If you don't allow her this privilege, you are denying her unfairly as well as denying yourself.

The high levels of pleasure possible with ESO can be achieved only with a partner's stimulation. They can't be achieved if the man is actively taking or controlling but only by giving up control. Difficulty with giving up control is a resistance, to be dealt with like any other resistance. (For further discussion see Chapter VIII, "Overcoming Resistances," p. 141.)

Differences—Controlling the Two-Stage Reflex

Male ESO is different from female ESO. In female ESO you moved up to and through brief orgasm to a higher level of orgasm. In male ESO a man moves up to and into first-stage orgasm: the emission stage, where there is hard erection, obvious arousal, and an intermittent secretion of clear fluid from the penis, which signals the presence of highly pleasurable internal contractions.

These contractions are from the prostate and other glands that contribute to semen production. You will help your partner reach this stage and extend it to even higher levels of arousal *without cresting over into ejaculation.*

The Prostate—A Man's Hidden Trigger

The role of the prostate gland in male sexual response has largely been ignored. Most men and their partners don't realize that stimulating this organ can add significantly to sexual arousal. We will discuss prostate stimulation in some detail in this chapter. Here we'd just like to explain why that stimulation is important.

Stimulating the male prostate is similar in some ways to stimulating the female G-spot area. Both areas have a similar nerve supply. Both areas may derive anatomically from the same fetal tissue. The G spot is still a subject of study. Of the existence and function of the prostate gland there is no doubt whatsoever.

Stimulating the prostate along with stimulating the penis produces a deeper, more powerful, longer orgasm in most men. Prolonged stimulation results in greater semen volume, and semen volume is one important factor in a man's sense of the intensity of his orgasm. Alternately or simultaneously stroking the penis and the prostate also produces high levels of continuous arousal. That's very much like the pattern of stimulation we described for women that involved alternately or simultaneously stimulating the clitoris and the vagina.

Some couples may want to experiment with direct prostate stimulation. A woman can stimulate her partner's prostate directly by inserting a lubricated finger into the rectum and pressing upward toward the scrotum. (See the illustration "Male Anatomy" for guidance.)

Positions

As you did before when it was your turn to be pleasured, your male partner now finds a comfortable position lying on his back. He props his head on a pillow if he likes. He separates his legs. You then have several options.

You can sit facing him between his legs with his legs flexed, knees up, and his thighs resting over yours. You may sit on your haunches, or cross your legs, or extend your legs. That allows both your hands access to his genitals. (See illustration number 7.)

Or, with your partner on his back, you can stretch out on your stomach or side, perpendicular to him—so that the two of you make a T—with your head and hands at the level of his genitals. You may be up on your elbow over his thigh, or he can rest his thigh over your body. In this position you have both hands free; you can also easily add oral stimulation. (See illustration number 10.)

Or you can start from a position sitting sideways between your partner's flexed legs. His legs are between or on top of your thighs. This position also makes it possible to add oral stimulation as well as manual. (See illustration number 4.)

Finally, and especially later in your ESO training, you can use a modified sixty-nine position, both of you resting on your sides turned toward each other with your heads at the level of each other's genitals. If your upper legs are flexed, each of you can then alternate manual as well as oral stimulation. You can take turns being cause and being effect or you can stimulate each other simultaneously. (See illustration number 5.)

It's important to be comfortable, otherwise you won't give your partner your full attention. Feel free to shift position when you begin to feel uncomfortable—to bend your legs more or less, to prop your elbow, to add or subtract a pillow. Shifting positions also changes the stimulation and helps your partner maintain ejaculatory control. Moving around is part of your sexual dance together. Try to continue genital stimulation even while you are moving to another position to reduce the distraction.

These are good, basic starting positions. From them you can both move easily into variations.

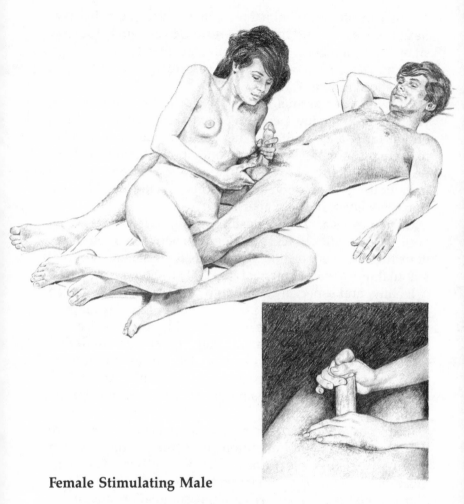

Female Stimulating Male

(4) Between Legs, Elbow Outside
Good access to genitals with hands and mouth. Left hand stimulates penis, right hand stimulates external prostate spot, testicles, and scrotum. Allows intimate eye contact. In easy variation, woman shifts body downward, still resting on elbow.

Inset shows double-ring stretch stroke.

Achieving Erection

Your partner won't necessarily have an erection at first. The reason he won't is that he's been paying attention to you, not to himself. He'll be aroused, but it's a myth, and a destructive one, that men automatically become erect in sexual situations. They don't. Most need their penises directly stimulated to achieve erection, especially men beyond their twenties who have been with a familiar partner for a few years. That's not a sign of inadequacy. It's normal. Men who are immediately erect without penile stimulation in every sexual encounter make up only a small minority of the general population.

Once you and your partner are comfortably positioned, you should proceed to do whatever you usually do to stimulate him to erection. One obvious thing you can do is to apply lubrication.

If, in the course of stimulating your partner, you plan to stimulate him orally, we suggest you do not use petrolatum now. Petrolatum tastes like . . . petrolatum. It lasts a long time, but it has neither a gourmet flavor nor texture. Use Albolene or our homemade lubricant recipe and add flavoring if you prefer.

Lubricate the penis thoroughly, as well as the scrotum, the perineum, and the external anal area. Lubricate both your hands. Use plenty of lubricant. Too much is better than too little. The preejaculatory fluid that men produce is insufficient for lubrication.

Begin now to stroke your partner's penis, remembering what you learned from him during Sexual Exploration training about the strokes he prefers. The basic manual stroke finds your dominant hand circling the glans of the penis with the thumb emphasizing the lip. Strong pressure and a heavy stroke are often best at the beginning. Most of the nerve endings in the penis are concentrated in the glans.

Remember, the glans is like your clitoris. It's a small area but very sensitive to stroking and pressure.

The Double-Ring Stretch Stroke

This is an excellent stroke to use to coax a reluctant penis into full erection, as well as to harden an already full one. (See illustration number 4.) Make a ring with the thumb and index finger of each hand, one above the other, around the shaft of the penis at its base. Use enough pressure to constrict some of the outflow of blood from the penis. If your left hand is ringed around the penis base, move your right hand ring upward toward the head of the penis. Then remove your right hand and again place two fingers in a ring just above your left hand near the base and again pull upward. Be sure to use enough pressure to trap some blood above your fingers and to stretch the penis as you stroke it. Develop a rhythm. You may find it useful to add a twisting motion to the stroke as your fingers move up the shaft. Another variant is repeatedly starting both hands in a ring around the middle of the shaft of the penis (rather than near the base) and moving them in opposite directions, one toward the base and the other toward the penis head. As the penis gets fuller, more than two fingers may be used to form the rings. To avoid fatigue, you may switch hands. The important thing is to move the rings up and down the shaft away from each other.

You should also experiment. Let your partner's penis be your guide. If his penis is hardening and stiffening, you're doing fine. But don't stop until you have given him a few minutes to respond. He may be working through resistance and need more time.

(5) Mutual Stimulation
Man and woman both lie on sides, resting on elbows, facing partner's genitals. Full manual/oral stimulation possible. Good for teaching and learning at same time.

Adding Stimulation

When he's arrived at full, hard erection and stayed that way for at least fifteen minutes, you can begin to stimulate your partner's scrotum and the area closer to the anus, behind the base of the scrotum—the perineum—where it's possible to push in without pressing against bone. The prostate gland is located inside your partner's body directly above that area. For convenience we'll refer to that external area as the "external prostate spot" from now on. (See the illustration "Male Anatomy.")

Pressure on the external prostate spot usually isn't comfortable until a man is fully aroused and his scrotum is elevated and hard. Then stimulation there can cause additional arousal.

So you can add to your partner's pleasure by caressing his scrotal and external prostate areas in several ways.

One involves pulling the scrotum (not jerking; pulling). Women usually avoid handling their partner's testicles. They've been taught that the testicles are extremely sensitive and can be easily hurt. Under other circumstances that's true, but during sexual arousal they enlarge and engorge and sensitivity to pain becomes, within limits, sensitivity to pleasure.

The testicles still shouldn't be squeezed, but they can be pulled, along with the entire scrotum. Don't hold on to the testicles themselves when you pull them. Make a loose clamp of your thumb and first fingers above the testicles on the scrotum, closer to the body, and apply traction that way. Or take firm hold of the scrotum with thumb and forefinger deeply *between* the testicles and pull. This method also works. You can pull lightly in rhythm either way as you stroke your partner's penis. (See illustration number 6.)

Scrotal pulling has another value. It's an excellent way to help your partner avoid ejaculating. Males usually don't

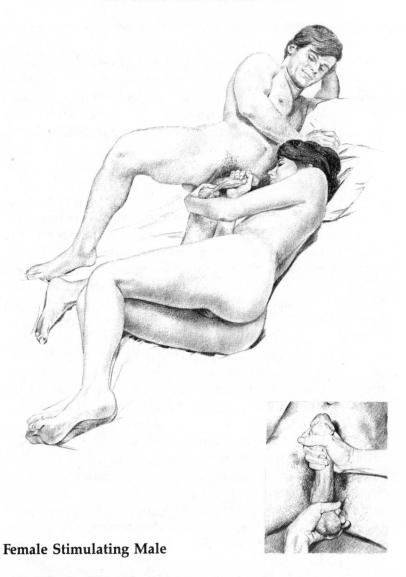

Female Stimulating Male

(6) **Side by Side**
   Woman's right hand on penis; left hand applies
   scrotal pull. Inset shows detail of scrotal pull for
   stimulation and for ejaculation control.

ejaculate until their testicles are fully drawn up against their bodies.

While you're applying scrotal traction you can lightly tease the penis by tickling the glans with a circle of fingers. You're pulling on your partner's scrotum to stop him from ejaculating, so you need to lighten stroking his penis. Teasing the glans can add to arousal even while you're holding your partner back from going over the top.

Another way to caress your partner is by applying pressure with one or two fingers (with well-trimmed nails) to his external prostate spot. Steady pressure feels good. So does stroking pressure in rhythm with stroking his penis. How hard you should press depends on how aroused he is. The more aroused, the more pressure is comfortable. Watch your partner's response. If you're applying too much pressure, he'll pull away. If he wants more, he'll move toward you. Many men complain that their partners are *too* gentle when handling their genitals. Don't be afraid to experiment.

A third caress we call the "prostate pincher." You can do it two different ways. Either press the forefinger of your dominant hand into your partner's external prostate spot, with the thumb of the same hand anchored hooked around the base of his penis; or reverse the position of the digits, anchor your forefinger around the base of the penis, and push in on the external prostate spot with your thumb. (See illustration number 7 and inset.) One method works better for some people, the other for others. If your prostate-pushing forefinger needs more support, you can back it up with your middle finger. Either way, stroke your partner's penis with your other hand at the same time. The more pressure on the external prostate spot and the faster the stroking, the faster the climb to arousal.

With continued, climbing stimulation, your partner will approach ejaculation. You don't want him to ejaculate, or his orgasm will end until he can return through the refractory

Female Stimulating Male

(7) Kneeling Between Legs
Good manual access. Woman can add oral
stimulation by bending over. Intimate eye contact.
Illustration and inset show left hand stimulating
penis, right hand applying prostate pincher with
thumb anchored at upper base of penis and index
finger pressing on external prostate spot below.

period to arousal. At this point do *not* stimulate the glans of the penis. Concentrate instead on other genital areas.

You have several means of control. One is the scrotal pull. A second is pressure on the external prostate spot, which distracts him. A third is squeezing firmly at the base of the penis with the forefinger in front and the thumb in back. A fourth is simply stopping stimulation. It may be necessary to take your hands away entirely. Stop stroking and simply pause, hands on or off, until his arousal decreases slightly, which may take only a few seconds or as much as a minute. Then begin stimulating him again. Try all these control techniques. Alternate them. See which combinations work best.

Controlling Ejaculation

At first you and your partner will have to pay close attention to controlling ejaculation. When you bring him up to the high level of arousal near ejaculation, he'll feel close to going over. You have to be very careful then, watching his signs of arousal and stopping or lightening and changing stimulation when he gets too close. Watch for his hands moving toward his genitals to push you away. Listen for changes in his sounds.

The man, for his part, is also working at control. He pulls away from your stroking. He shifts mental attention away from his sensation. Or he uses Kegel exercises to help with control.

There'll be slips along the way. It's like learning how to ski or roller-skate—you fall a lot at first. The man should enjoy his orgasm when it happens by relaxing and letting go. Then you both should discuss the experience to find out why it happened and to plan for more effective control. The primary responsibility for control at this point is yours.

Just as women do, men contract their pelvic muscles to build arousal. When your partner feels ejaculation approaching, one way he can regain control is to hold his breath momentarily and push his pelvic muscles out—bearing down. This process is like straining for a moment to move his bowels. Breath holding and bearing down can momentarily stop the climb to ejaculation. Combining squeezing the pelvic muscles even tighter—holding in—with breath holding may also be effective. Then it's up to you to reduce the stimulation momentarily until your partner regains ejaculatory control.

Some men find deliberate, slow, deep breathing or, contrarily, faster panting helps control ejaculation. They may combine deliberate, slow breathing with bearing down, or deliberate, slow breathing with clenching. Each man must determine for himself the most effective combination of breath holding, deliberate breathing, and tightening or relaxing of the pelvic muscles.

It's important to remember that the man's ejaculation *isn't* your goal. In ESO, when your partner approaches ejaculation, you should *reduce* stimulation, not increase it.

Having regained control by bearing down while you reduced stimulation, your partner can now maintain control as you begin stroking again by again contracting his pelvic muscles. It's a question of shifting attention. Anything that shifts your partner's attention will momentarily level him off.

Control becomes a matter of teamwork: you sense his level of arousal and change rhythm and stroke to help him with control; at the same time, he responds with muscular contractions and relaxations and by bearing down. In the first stage of ESO, men can never quite lose consciousness to the extent women can. This first ESO stage is still extremely pleasurable, and it's more pleasurable the more *you*, his partner, learn to take control of preventing ejaculation. In the second stage of ESO, control of ejaculation becomes more automatic. It proceeds without effort or anxiety, and a man feels as if he has entered an altered state of consciousness that can last as long as he and you wish.

If he is becoming more and more aroused—climbing—his legs will usually flex more as his body reaches for stimulation. When he wants to level or come down to avoid ejaculating, he will usually extend his legs and pull away. You must learn to read these motions accurately.

If you have agreed in advance on how much time you will spend stimulating your partner, don't change that agreement now. He may indicate by his arousal that he wants to ejaculate quickly. Don't encourage him or give in to his sense of urgency or pressure. If a man doesn't know about the much greater amount of pleasure possible in ESO, he pushes for ejaculation. You must be strong and help him resist this urge. If you give in too soon and stimulate him to ejaculation, you will be robbing him of greater pleasure, and he may feel responsible for failing to control himself.

Resistances

While you're building arousal, your partner will be working through resistances. They're the same resistances we listed before: worries about work, time, propriety, and distraction. Males also often have to deal with their chauvinisms:

> Am I letting her run me?
> Can she handle me?
> Can I trust her to do it right?

Or they may be dealing with their doubts:

> Is she really enjoying this?
> She must be getting tired.
> Am I reacting properly?

Men learning ESO have an additional and opposite problem from women learning ESO. Women mainly have to learn to let go. Men first must be able to let go, to allow arousal and erection, but then men have to learn *not* to let go, to prevent early ejaculation. For each sex the learning leads to greater pleasure. There's a promise of much more on the other side. Men who are hesitant to give up control should remember the reason for doing so: it feels good, and better and better.

So your male partner must deal with resistances somewhat differently from you. When he finds himself losing arousal because of resistances or any other distractions, he needs to turn his attention deliberately inward again to sensation. *He needs to concentrate and reconcentrate on sensation, adding the control mechanism of Kegel exercises.* Cognitive restructuring doesn't work as well for the man because he needs to monitor his state of arousal continually at first to avoid ejaculating. If he switches to a positive thought or repeats a neutral phrase, the sensation can catch him by surprise.

Men need to pay attention to breathing. They also sometimes hold their breath while they're concentrating their muscles to build arousal. If they hold their breath too long, they lose control. Remind your partner to breathe if you notice him holding his breath for longer than about twenty seconds.

Sneaking Up

If you've tried everything else and your partner still resists, try making him *laugh*. At the same time keep stimulating his penis very rapidly and with hard strokes. Sneak up on him. Say something funny or kid him. Act silly. Make a face. He can't resist as much when he's laughing.

Achieving Male ESO

The graph titled "Male Orgasmic Responses" shows the differences in arousal and response through time of male single orgasm, multiple orgasm, and male ESO (Stage I, Stage II, Stage III).

In single orgasm (Stage I), arousal increases with stimulation through an excitement phase to a three- to five-second burst of pleasurable internal contractions (emission-state orgasm), which is experienced as a sense of ejaculatory inevitability—the point of no return. Your partner knows he's going to ejaculate and can't stop. Several seconds later ejaculation begins, with six to ten strong, propulsive orgasmic contractions and the expulsion of semen, lasting about ten seconds.

After a refractory period of several minutes or longer, when stimulation isn't effective, a man may have a second, similar orgasm. This is multiple orgasm in the male (Stage II).

In ESO (Stage III), the sense of ejaculatory inevitability is brought under control. The phase of pleasurable internal contractions increases from a few seconds to a minute, to ten minutes, even to thirty minutes or more. Ejaculation occurs when either partner chooses.

By learning to control the approach of ejaculatory inevitability, your partner will be able to accept increasing amounts of stimulation during emission-state orgasm. His level of arousal will increase. He'll experience the stimulation as increasingly pleasurable and he'll be able to accept more of it longer without ejaculating. He will still be using some ejaculatory control techniques himself—breathing, Kegel exercises, switching attention, for example. During this time he may secrete as much as an ounce or more of clear fluid that is thinner than semen. When he ejaculates, his ejaculatory orgasm will be more intense and will also last longer. Instead of six to ten contractions, there may be fifteen to twenty or more. This is especially true if the man has been practicing Kegel exercises and the testicle-elevation and semen-withholding exercises we described earlier.

Eventually, with ejaculation, the man trained in ESO also experiences a refractory period. But with mutual interest and continued, correct stimulation, he can reenter extended orgasm within several minutes or even seconds. His penis may be partly or fully erect then.

Your partner's general level of sexual arousal (and probably his levels of sexual hormones) will remain higher from day to day if you and he keep up your ESO skills. Then you'll find even brief sessions of lovemaking more pleasurable.

Training Schedule

During training make it your goal to take your partner to a peak of arousal close to ejaculation at least fifteen times, on the average, during a thirty-minute session. You'll find as you and he learn control that he'll stay at higher and higher levels between peaks. Eventually there won't be much decline between peaks and you'll be supplying only very light, subtle changes in pressure and rhythm.

Extended Sexual Orgasm

After a while, as your partner works through his resistances and as you both learn the teamwork of ejaculatory control, you'll find it easier and easier to stimulate him to very high levels of arousal. He'll find it easier and easier to stay there.

The intensely pleasurable state close to ejaculation becomes more stable with experience and extends in time, as we saw in the graph of male response. You begin to notice an intermittent secretion of fluid from your partner's penis. His penis is hard and engorged and it doesn't soften unless you completely stop stimulating. He's not thrusting or straining. You're the driver, controlling his level of arousal and maintaining him just this side of ejaculation. He's the passenger, along for the ride—he's giving up control to you. In the early stages of ESO he may show the same signs of extreme arousal that you showed—moaning, panting, sweating, jerking his arms and legs. He's testing your sensitivity to his level of arousal and his feelings. He's learning that your goal is not to push him over that point of no return, but instead to extend his pleasure.

In Phase II ESO he will become more stabilized. The jerking and panting tend to diminish as he experiences quieter ecstasy. His blood pressure and heart rate drop moderately from their high levels in earlier stages of orgasm. His pelvic muscles relax. His anal sphincter relaxes and opens.

Eventually his penis may become so sensitized that a light touch, a teasing tickle, even simply blowing warm air on it or applying cool lubricant to it and letting the lubricant melt, give intense pleasure.

Your partner is experiencing Phase II ESO. You can keep him there for as long as you both like.

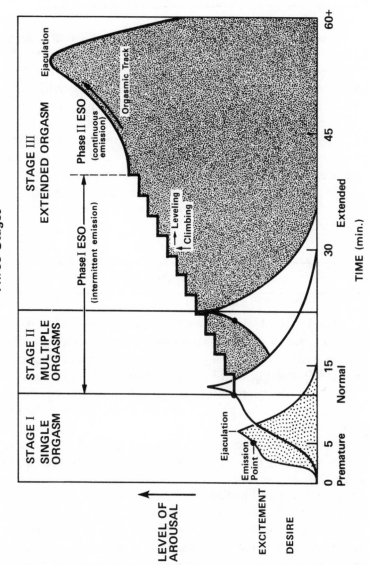

MALE ORGASMIC RESPONSES
Three Stages

Changing Stroking

When we discussed giving the woman pleasure, we said it was important for the man not to vary his stroking too much—some teasing, but not a lot of variation. The opposite is true for men. Steady, unvarying stroking will either reduce arousal or carry your partner straight to ejaculation. Because his ESO requires control, he needs lots of variety. Changing strokes prevents ejaculation. You may want to supply a steady, stimulating stroke when he's climbing to greater arousal. But change the stroking when he's close.

You'll find you need to change positions and switch hands for your own comfort. That has the added value of automatically changing the stroke.

Finishing

When you decide to end a session of ESO, take your partner on to ejaculation—if you both haven't decided to finish with intercourse—by giving him extra stimulation. Keep stimulating him lightly through ejaculation and afterward, paying more attention to his scrotum, his prostate, and the shaft of his penis when his glans becomes hypersensitive to touch.

If you keep stimulating after ejaculation appears to be over, you can extend ejaculatory orgasm by half a dozen contractions or more. You'll be *lightly* caressing the penis and pushing and milking the external prostate spot. Part of your partner's pleasure during ejaculation comes from the sensation of fluid pushing up from the base of the penis. By pushing on the external prostate spot you can mimic that good feeling. Then the pulsing of the deeper pelvic muscles can continue for several pleasurable minutes.

VII

ESO: MORE WAYS TO GIVE

Intercourse

The techniques you've just learned for male and female ESO are basic and central. They're ways to deeper levels of pleasure that should become a permanent part of your sexual repertoire. They're not a temporary substitute for intercourse or a supplement. They're not "variations." Extended sexual orgasm can best be learned when both partners pay attention to one sexual arousal at a time. In terms of levels of arousal, ESO by manual—and oral, which we'll talk about in this chapter—stimulation is more intense than intercourse that has not been preceded by manual stimulation. The blind, blunt penis, the mitten of the vagina, honorable apparatus that they are, can't initially match two skilled hands and a mouth.

That certainly doesn't mean you should abandon intercourse. Quite the contrary. Intercourse is an important part of ESO. These techniques, practiced at least once a week, are a desirable prerequisite to intercourse. If ESO by manual means is more intense than intercourse, it's also, necessarily, less intimate. Making love locked together in each other's arms is deeply satisfying emotionally and spiritually. The best possible lovemaking combines the intensity of manual/oral ESO with the intimacy of intercourse following. ESO continues into intercourse with even more intense contractions, making intercourse more pleasurable, less strenuous, more deeply satisfying, than ever before.

After each of you has pleasured the other to ESO, using manual or oral stimulation or both, you may want to move into intercourse. Even after a long period of ESO, partners often want to finish with intercourse—the grand finale.

If you've followed the pattern we've suggested—the man pleasuring the woman first, then the woman pleasuring the man—the woman will find it easy to return to a state of orgasmic arousal. The man's state will depend on whether or not his partner stimulated him to ejaculation. Even if he did ejaculate, he may find it easy to achieve another erection quickly and ejaculate again with intercourse, especially if he has been practicing Kegel exercises and semen-withholding exercises. Most men, up to at least their late forties, shouldn't have any difficulties. Older men may. That's a natural effect of aging. So, depending on a man's capacity, he may or may not elect to be stimulated to ejaculation at the end of a period of ESO. He may choose to save ejaculation for intercourse. Discuss arrangements beforehand, but don't worry if it doesn't go according to plan.

We've found that men trained in ESO are more capable of recovery after ejaculation, in less time, than they were before ESO training. Men who have regularly practiced semen withholding also have an advantage. Sometimes they have to push deliberately through the resistance of *thinking* they can't have a second—or third, or fourth—ejaculation. But there's nothing wrong with saving ejaculation for intercourse either. It feels wonderful then, and it guarantees the woman a hard erection to enjoy.

After ejaculation, the man should continue his thrusting movements, even if his penis becomes less hard. Remember, engorgement of the female genitals magnifies your partner's perception of size. Even a partially erect penis will feel extremely pleasurable and much larger than its actual dimensions. Just arrange to keep the softened penis inside the vagina during these continued thrusting motions.

Control Positions

Imaginative men and women in every country and of every age have invented hundreds of different positions for lovemaking. We won't even attempt to list them all. We do want to mention a few, to point out their advantages for control. Then you can have the pleasure together of assessing the others on your own.

Some positions allow the man to control movement and therefore to control the amount of stimulation he's receiving. Others allow the woman to control her movement and her stimulation. And others make it possible for a couple to pass control back and forth, or to control movement mutually.

The "missionary" position—the woman on her back, the man on top between her legs—is a male-control position. The man thrusts, and the woman's movement is restricted, yet it's a good position, which is why so many people use it. A small percentage of men find it a position useful to help delay ejaculation, especially men intimidated by a more aggressive position of female control. It allows couples to look at each other and hold each other intimately.

A corresponding position where the woman is most in control finds the man on his back and the woman kneeling astride him. Here she moves and his movement is restricted. In this position the woman can easily direct her partner's penis to stimulate her G spot. She can also rotate her pelvis to rub her clitoris directly against the base of her partner's penis. Many men resist this position. They falsely equate female control with emotional domination. But this is a good position for learning ejaculatory control.

Both partners kneeling with the man behind the woman (or the woman kneeling on a bed and the man standing on the floor) allows mutual control. (See illustration number 8.) The man may thrust; the woman may sway forward and back on her hands and knees or her forearms and knees; they both may move together. The man's penis can easily be angled to press against and stimulate the woman's inner trigger area.

A modification of the missionary position is also good for stimulating the G spot: the woman, on her back, positions a small, thick pillow beneath her buttocks to tilt the front of her pelvis up, increasing the angle of contact between her vagina and her partner's penis. The man mounts on top between her legs.

For prolonged intercourse, a side-scissors position can reduce fatigue. (See illustration number 9.) This position also makes it easier for the woman to stimulate her partner manually during intercourse. The woman lies on her back, turned halfway on her right side (if she's right-handed); the man inserts his penis while he's between his partner's legs in the missionary position, then moves his left leg over her right leg so that his legs scissor her right leg and his perineal area is exposed. Her right hand is then free to stimulate his external prostate spot, the buried root of his penis, and behind his testicles, and to control his urge to ejaculate with a scrotal pull.

Men who have good ejaculatory control report that when they have intercourse they make frequent *subtle* adjustments in their movements. These adjustments may include slightly speeding up or slowing down their thrusting, changing their angle of penetration, or syncopating their rhythm. Doing Kegel exercises also helps increase control—tightening, relaxing, and pushing out.

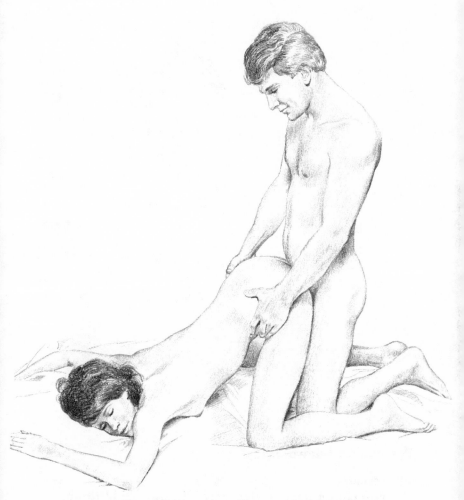

Position for Intercourse

(8) Rear Entry
   Mutual control. Woman can rotate pelvis for
   maximum stimulation, including G-spot stimulation.
   Deep penetration possible.

Position for Intercourse

(9) Scissors

Woman on back, rolled partly to side, right thigh between man's legs. Man on side, supporting himself on right shoulder, right thigh between woman's legs. Both partners position hips for free movement. Good for prolonged intercourse with little effort. Mutual control.

After enjoying intercourse for ten minutes to half an hour or more, depending on your desire and your energy levels, you may wish to conclude by taking each other to a peak of pleasure. Do this by increasing the depth and speeding up the rate of your thrusting. At this point the man may choose to ejaculate. Both of you please remember to vocalize your pleasure during your finale; it will give you an extra boost.

Intercourse with a soft penis can be useful and pleasurable when a couple bypasses oral or manual ESO and the man is not erect but wishes to proceed directly to intercourse. See "Soft Penis Intercourse," p. 176, for a description of this technique. Illustration number 12 demonstrates it.

Women who regularly practice ESO often experience rapid orgasmic response with intercourse. When ESO is a regular part of a couple's practice—at least once or twice a week—natural lubrication and rapid orgasmic response may occur within a minute of penetration and thrusting. Women who don't always naturally lubricate quickly should use a lubricant to facilitate rapid orgasm. The rear-entry position, illustration number 11, works well. The woman should *push out*, opening the vagina to the penis and allowing her to accept penetration and find it immediately arousing. Rapid orgasmic response turns the "quickie" from an insult into a pleasure. The memory of recent ESO allows a woman to reproduce that ESO experience with minimal foreplay.

Couples often find themselves routinely making love in the same position week after week. That's fine as long as it's a deliberate choice among other positions, communicated and agreed upon. But choosing other positions for lovemaking can be useful, and arousing, from time to time, to see what new pleasures you can find in them. You don't necessarily need a book. You can make up your own. Fantasize about what you might like, then discuss your ideas with your partner and experiment.

Oral Lovemaking

You can increase pleasure two ways: by feeling more intensely through the channels of pleasure you already know and by opening up new channels. The entire surface of your body is a sensing organ. It feels. It can learn to feel more. That's not oversubtlety or mysticism. That's simple fact.

Oral lovemaking—genital "kissing"—can be a source of great pleasure. It isn't necessary to ESO, as we've mentioned. It adds. Combined with manual stimulation, it adds intensity and improves control. It's an additional channel and a delightful one.

Some men and women strongly resist oral lovemaking, or haven't yet included it in their sexual repertoire. For a discussion of oral techniques, see "Learning Oral Lovemaking," p. 208.

For men and women who already enjoy oral sex, we offer the following suggestions.

Women:
Orally stimulating your partner's penis during ESO can lift him to higher levels of arousal. Kneeling between his legs is one comfortable position for oral sex. (See illustration number 7.) While continuing manual stimulation, you may want to shift his body and yours so that you are both lying on your sides, facing each other, with your head at the level of his penis. Rest your head on a pillow. You'll be able to continue stimulating your partner manually, including his penis, his scrotum, and his prostate, while adding oral stimulation to his penis. (See illustration number 6.)

Another position you can shift to is lying on your side with your head between his legs, resting on his thigh, with his body partly turned toward you and his free leg flexed over your body. (See illustration number 2.)

Or try lying on your side with your elbow outside his thigh. (See illustration number 10.) This position gives access to his entire genital area. The illustration shows one hand pulling on the scrotum, which for many men increases arousal and helps to control ejaculation.

Either way, you can use whatever oral techniques your partner finds arousing—licking the shaft of his penis, mouthing the glans while you continue stroking the shaft with your hands, moving your head up and down on the glans and as much of the shaft as you can comfortably take into your mouth.

Experiment. If you stimulate your partner to a high level of arousal by hand before you begin oral lovemaking, he won't be thrusting now. If he is, he's asking for more stimulation, which you can best increase manually. At peak levels of sensation you'll need only the lightest touch with mouth and tongue. That's when oral stimulation works best with ESO.

Men usually prefer heavier stimulation than women, both manually and orally. Women tend to stimulate a male too gently and then hold him responsible for not achieving erection. If your partner has trouble achieving erection with oral stimulation, it may be because you aren't stimulating him vigorously enough for long enough periods of time to help him through his resistances. Once he knows that you are able to stimulate him through his resistances to full erection and that you intend to do just that no matter how much he resists, he will let go of resistance more quickly and allow himself to become erect.

To stimulate erection, experiment with stronger pressure and more rapid oral and manual strokes. Add pressure with your hands on the shaft of your partner's penis and with your mouth on the glans. Surround the entire glans with your mouth. Protect the penis from your teeth by covering them with your lips. Move your head rapidly up and down and simultaneously stroke the penile shaft with your lubricated hand. The motion of your hand on the shaft should

Female Stimulating Male

(10) **Lying on Side, Elbow Outside Thigh**
 **Left hand stimulates penis; right hand uses scrotal
 pull for stimulation and for ejaculation control.
 Comfortable oral access.**

follow the motion of your mouth, as if your hand were a continuation of your mouth. This technique feels like deep-throating: as if you were encompassing the entire penis in your mouth.

Your other hand can simultaneously stimulate the external prostate area. That stimulation—pressing inward and up-ward toward the penis, stroking as if squeezing fluid from the prostate gland inside—need not necessarily be coordi-nated with the rhythm of oral stimulation.

Your partner may not become aroused and erect the moment you begin stimulating him. He may need ten min-utes or thirty minutes to let go of resistances and to clear away intrusive thoughts. This time corresponds to the time of continuous, reliable stimulation that many women need to achieve Stage I orgasm. So you should prepare yourself in terms both of physical comfort and of personal determina-tion to provide strong, effective oral stimulation for up to half an hour, even if your partner's penis doesn't become erect during most of that time. You'll need to change hands and vary strokes to avoid getting tired. If your jaw becomes tired, take your mouth off the glans. Substitute a well-lubricated hand on the glans alone. Use a squeezing, pull-ing, and milking stroke to create a mild suctionlike sensation. Your other hand should continue to stroke the shaft rhythmically. Along the way you might remind your-self of how long you take to let go of resistance when it's your turn to be stimulated.

Once your partner is fully erect and nearing ejaculation, you'll want to lighten stimulation. That sustains arousal without encouraging ejaculation. You'll need to stimulate only very lightly with your mouth and your tongue during ESO. When you notice arousal dropping even slightly—penis softening, testicles lowering, preejaculatory fluid stop-ping—immediately increase oral and manual stimulation by adding pressure and speeding up the stroke.

Your partner's testicles as well as his penis are sensitive to oral stimulation. You can lightly stimulate his testicles, one at a time, by taking one into your mouth and gently moving your tongue around it. Stimulate the scrotum as well: use your lips to pull on the scrotum while your lubricated hands stimulate the penile shaft and glans.

Deep-throating, the technique Linda Lovelace made famous in the notorious film, isn't difficult to learn and can be an exciting variation in oral technique.

Most women find that taking more than an inch or two of penis into their mouth triggers the gag reflex in a plexus of nerves at the upper back of their throat. To control your gag reflex, simply *swallow* when you feel the urge to gag. Don't be afraid. You won't swallow your partner's penis. Instead, swallowing constricts your throat and stimulates the penile glans.

Deep-throating your partner's penis blocks your breathing, so take a good breath first. When you need to exhale, move the penis out of your throat back into your mouth. Breathe, then take the penis in deeply again. By alternating these two motions you set up a stroke. You hold your breath for five or ten seconds with your partner's penis deep in your throat, blocking breathing. Then you slide the penis out of your throat, still keeping the glans fully in your mouth, and exhale, breathe, slide the penis as deep into your throat as you can take it (keeping your neck extended and straight helps), and slide the penis out again. You can continue for as long as your partner finds the process pleasurable and you find it comfortable.

Men:
Especially at higher levels of arousal, women usually prefer lighter rather than harder stimulation. *Most men use too much pressure.* Heavy suction, pressure, or motion may quickly become uncomfortable. Men probably overstimulate because they like strong stimulation themselves and assume their partners feel the same way. They're wrong. In our experi-

Male Stimulating Female

(11) **Kneeling Over**
   Oral access to genitals. Free hand may stimulate
   breasts and other body areas. In minor variation,
   man extends legs and lies on stomach.

ence most complaints from women about manual and oral technique concern roughness. Even if a woman has told her partner to lighten up, she shouldn't be afraid to remind him each time he stimulates her uncomfortably and incorrectly. She should be tactful, but you should be receptive. When your partner's clitoris is erect and hard it requires only very light stimulation.

Regular, predictable, rhythmic stimulation is good basic technique. Explore with your tongue to find the most sensitive areas on and around your partner's clitoris, then alternate tongue stimulation with suction, pushing with your tongue and then lightly sucking the clitoris into your mouth. Experiment with rapidly flicking your tongue. The most effective pressure is sometimes so light that you'll make hardly any contact between your mouth and your partner's vulva. Your mouth's warmth and the motion of the air from your breathing may be enough to stimulate her arousal for seconds at a time.

Your mouth and tongue effectively replace one hand when you switch to oral lovemaking during ESO. Your other hand can continue to stimulate the vagina, especially the G spot. You can alternate primary stimulation between the clitoris and the G spot just as you did with your hands before.

As always, let your partner's responses guide you. If she is climbing to arousal, continue whatever you have found that is stimulating her. If she is leveling off or coming down from arousal, change what you are doing. Try stimulating the clitoris less. Or try stimulating the clitoris more. Or add more or less G-spot stimulation.

The important rule to remember is to change stimulation when you sense that your partner is coming down from arousal. Sometimes what you have to change is your attention. If you're thinking of something else while you're stimulating your partner, she may unconsciously sense your distraction and respond by becoming less aroused. Pay attention to your partner at all times.

Men and women:

Be alert for resistances to oral sex (see Chapter VIII, "Overcoming Resistances," p. 141). Talk about them before you begin. If you encounter them during lovemaking, talk them out afterward. A good rule to follow is that either partner should feel free to signal a return to regular lovemaking or to manual ESO whenever he or she becomes uncomfortable, physically or emotionally, with oral sex.

VIII

OVERCOMING RESISTANCES

W E BEGAN talking about resistances in Chapters V and
VI. In this chapter we'll discuss them in more detail.

Resistances are the mental conditions, conscious and unconscious, that determine what experiences we allow ourselves to have. They include the attitudes, the rigidities, the
rules, the fears, and the misinformation that limit our ability
to experience more pleasure. Everyone has sexual resistances, or all of us would automatically experience extended
orgasm the first time we were aroused. You're aware of
some of your resistances. Others—probably the majority—
you're unaware of. Some resistance is normal and essential
to survival.

The first step toward overcoming specific resistances is
identifying them. The simplest way to do that is to make a
list. The resistances you're aware of you can identify easily.
The ones you're unaware of you'll have to discover as you go
along.

Religious Prohibitions

Many people encounter resistances connected to past or present religious prohibitions. You must finally decide if any form of sexual pleasuring violates your faith, and, if so, whether or not you want to accept that prohibition and the limitation on pleasure it enforces.

You should be aware that all religions and all societies have arranged to control sexuality, usually by limiting it to specified acts and partners. The key word is *control*. The basic purpose of that control is to remind you of the religion or society and to demonstrate your voluntary respect for its power. In an intimate, strongly emotional context like sexuality, a rule restricting you from making love in a certain position, for example, forcefully recalls you to your faith and emphasizes the reach of that faith into the most private center of your life.

Unfortunately, some men and women who learned religious prohibitions as children find themselves inhibited as adults. They find they've emotionally generalized specific rules until all of sexuality is permeated with a sense of sin, even sexuality permitted within the context of their faith and even, in some cases, after they've given that faith up.

If that's a serious problem for you, you may need to consider undergoing short-term psychotherapy. If you discover more specific and limited religion-based resistances, the techniques for overcoming resistances we'll discuss here should work for you.

Resistance to self-stimulation in particular can be a religion-based anxiety. Besides the relaxation techniques we'll discuss here, the best way we know to work through that resistance is to realize that you aren't learning self-stimulation only for yourself. You're learning it to improve your relationship with your partner, to improve your ability to give and receive pleasure, to add to intimacy and commitment. In any religion, intention is crucial in judging behavior. The intention of the self-stimulation exercises here, which serve as a kind of extended foreplay, is to strengthen your bond of love with your partner.

Dealing with Children

Another resistance that plagues many men and women is concern for what their children know and hear of their lovemaking. Children of every age can severely inhibit couples trying to arrange time and privacy for lovemaking. Fear that children can hear them can paralyze parents. Anxiety that time set aside for pleasure is time stolen from children can make sex furtive and all too brief.

The children problem breaks down into several separate problems with different solutions.

You can usually arrange time for sex while very young children and infants are sleeping, since they sleep so many hours. Infants up to the age of perhaps eight months can even sleep in the same room if neither of you finds that inhibiting, thus eliminating the worry that they've waked and you've failed to hear them.

Older children need first to be provided for. You need to do whatever must be done—dinner served, assistance supplied with homework, transportation arranged—to convince yourselves that your children are fine and you're not shirking parenting by pleasuring each other. If providing for your children consistently gets in the way of private time together, then you need to discuss rearranging and simplifying your schedules. No matter how demanding your responsibilities as parents appear to be, *all* parents need, and must take, some private time to devote exclusively to each other. Your children will benefit in the long run.

Tell children why you're leaving them alone: "Mommy

and Daddy need time by themselves to enjoy and love each other." The important word is *love*. Children feel safer when they know their parents love each other.

If your child's response is "Why do you and Daddy need private time? Why can't I be there? I love you too," then one answer is "When we can give each other love privately, we feel closer and that helps us love *you* more too." Another answer is "Everyone gets a turn. Sometimes I'm just with you. Sometimes Daddy's just with you. Sometimes I'm just with Daddy."

Another question children ask that the word *love* helps answer: "Why were you crying when you and Daddy were alone? Was Daddy hurting you?" You answer: "Those were love sounds. Daddy and I make them when we're loving each other a whole lot." The child understands that you weren't in pain and learns that vocalizing during lovemaking is good. If the thought of being overheard is personally inhibiting, you can always mask your vocalizing with music.

Sooner or later children test their parents' resolve to be alone. All those little knocks on the door. You can help forestall them, and allay the guilt you may feel about them, by giving the child loving attention before the door is closed. But when you hear the knock and the call, be definite. Tell the child you meant it when you said you were having private time. You don't want to be disturbed. The child can do whatever you arranged beforehand for him to do—watch TV, nap, go out and play. You'll be with him again in half an hour, an hour. Not "in a minute," unless that's literally true. Then follow through. Afterward give the child extra attention to show him that he's loved.

Once you've dealt with the little knocks, you may have to deal with the resistance of your overconcern: "I really should stop now." Use the techniques developed in this chapter. And remind yourself that you can give your children far more love when you have a strong, fulfilling relationship with your partner and feel good about yourself than when you don't. After ESO time especially, you're likely to return happy and relaxed to caring for your children.

Common Resistances

All resistances are partly thought and partly feeling. They won't instantly disappear if you change the thought. They also have to be worked through emotionally, and that takes time. But to the extent that they're based on misinformation and bad communication, you can start working through them by rethinking them. In Chapter V we listed a few common resistances. Here's that list again, with additions and with some discussion:

1. *My partner's getting tired.* If you've agreed ahead of time that each of you will stop when you feel tired, trust your partner to keep the agreement. In the meantime enjoy yourself. There's nothing wrong with going ahead even when you're tired, by the way. Sometimes that pushes through resistances and generates a welcome sense of achievement.

2. *I don't have time.* Arrange time in advance. Remember, if you want to learn ESO you must give sex higher priority than you probably have in the past.

3. *I feel silly.* That's because you're doing something new. Do it anyway. When it's familiar to you, you won't feel silly anymore. Silliness can be fun if you let it be. Watch how children play.

4. *I look unattractive.* Women have this worry more than men, but it's not uncommon among men. You like your partner's sounds and movements and expressions in love-making. You like your partner's body. Why assume that your partner doesn't like yours? If you need reassurance, ask for it. If you think your partner wants reassurance, offer it: "You're beautiful." "You're sexy." "You're wonderful." For

people who love each other, one or more of those statements is bound to be true.

5. *I have my period.* You can practice ESO during menstruation if both of you find that practice comfortable. Discuss it and agree in advance, then trust your partner to have been honest in his agreement.

ESO during menstruation may decrease the number of days and the volume of flow. The intense and prolonged uterine contractions of extended orgasm help move the menstrual material more efficiently from the uterus. A towel will protect the sheets.

6. *I'm angry.* Why? If it's old anger, leave it outside the bedroom door and discuss it in communication exercises at neutral times. If it's anger that came up during lovemaking, deal with it like any other resistance, using the techniques we consider in this chapter and in Chapters V and VI.

Other thoughts you can similarly reason out with yourself include: *I'm afraid./ I feel like I'm going to burst./ This is wrong./ Tomorrow I've got to . . . / Yesterday I should have . . . / I don't think I can do this.*

Changing Behavior

Behavior arises in thought and feeling. Resistance is one kind of behavior. Given time and attention, any behavior can be changed. At our clinic in California we help people with smoking, weight control, blood-pressure control, headaches, asthma, chronic pain, alcohol and drug dependency, sleep disturbances, bed-wetting, muscle tics and spasms, depression, anxiety, anger, phobias, dieting, sexual problems, and more. What can't be changed can at least be modified.

Many of the same methods of change work for all these problems. Anxiety is part of almost all unwanted behavior, so we help people free themselves from anxiety. Misinformation or lack of information usually complicates unwanted behavior, so we help people reeducate themselves. Behavior can usually best be changed in small, incremental steps rather than all at once, so we devise and supervise programs of gradual readjustment. And what applies to the relief of pain and unhappiness applies equally well to the relief of unhappy and sometimes painful resistances to increasing sexual pleasure.

Desi is a former client we remember with great fondness. He was a successful thirty-four-year-old businessman from India who had lived in the United States for five years when we first saw him. He was charming and humble; he was also a virgin. He had self-stimulated three or four times when he was fourteen; that was the extent of his sexual experience. He was extremely anxious because his parents had arranged a marriage for him and he was sure he'd be a failure on his wedding night. He wasn't aware of having erections and he had very little interest in sex, but he wanted to learn.

We began at the beginning with education. Desi was raised in a religious culture that taught that sex is evil. His parents had punished him severely when he was a child for playing doctor with his friends. We reminded him that he was conceived through sexual intercourse and entered the world through a sexual orifice. Could sex be so evil, we asked him, if nearly all of us depend on it for our very lives?

We showed Desi training films, instructed him in self-stimulation techniques, reduced his anxiety with hypnosis and biofeedback, taught him to fantasize. In time he was able to produce strong, sustained erections and had mastered full information about how to stimulate his bride-to-be. He needed then to practice what he knew, but he lacked a partner. Since his marriage was arranged, and his future bride was therefore a stranger, far away in another country, we encouraged Desi to work with a surrogate—a woman trained in sex therapy who was willing to help him learn. He agreed. He and the surrogate progressed through five meetings from simply talking and touching to full, satisfying intercourse. In their last meetings Desi was able to stimulate the surrogate to extended orgasm for as much as ten minutes at a time.

Desi went home to his arranged marriage. We heard from him once more. He wrote us that he and his wife were both very happy with his sexual skills.

Controlling Thought

We talked earlier about controlling your thoughts—"cognitive restructuring"—when you encounter a resistance (see p. 89 for review). It takes about three seconds, after a thought arises in the brain, to identify the thought content, to decide to change it, and to make the change. We've watched the process in our office in clients attached to biofeedback equipment. Their galvanic skin response, which is a sensitive measure of emotional arousal, suddenly changes. The equipment registers the change with an audible tone and the meters jump. The client hears the tone and says "Yes, I did just have a thought. I was wondering if I can handle this training."

At that point the client can change his response most simply by reversing the thought: instead of thinking "I'm really scared," he can deliberately think "I'm really comfortable. I can handle it." Instead of "This is terrible," he can think "This is exciting." *Even if he doesn't believe it.* People finally believe what they choose to believe, what they tell themselves to believe. That's why coaches give pep talks and politicians make appearances to the crescendo of a band playing "Happy Days Are Here Again." In the context of our work a client's deliberate reversal of a thought is founded on a provisional truth: "I'm really comfortable" is what he *hopes* to be and what he *will be* after successful training.

Reversing negative thoughts works well in sexual situations. You should tell yourself "I like being pleasured," "I feel good." Your partner can encourage you too. Make a habit of using such phrases as a bridge to feeling good.

A second way to move past a point of resistance, mentioned earlier, is to replace a distracting thought with a neutral thought. The neutral thought can be a nonsense sound: "Ahhh." "Ommm." It can be a phrase: "I'm calm." "My mind is quiet." Repeated over and over, mantras such as these push distracting thoughts aside. Like solid objects, two thoughts can't occupy the same space in consciousness at the same time. A neutral mantra allows your body's natural responses to reassert themselves. When you're being sexually stimulated, that means a greater sensation of pleasure.

A third way to restructure thoughts, we said earlier, is to switch your attention inward to *feeling* and allow the physical experience of being stimulated to take over your awareness.

Paying attention to feeling means just that: paying attention to your body and the sensation that your partner is creating for you. Some people resist pleasure by telling themselves that their partners aren't stimulating them correctly. Assuming that their partners aren't causing them pain, and assuming they've taught their partners what feels good, that expectation is probably misguided. One kind of stimulation may feel better than another, but *you can take any amount of stimulation and use it to build arousal by paying attention to it*. Every time you find yourself thinking—especially negative thoughts—switch your attention back to sensation.

We've treated preorgasmic women—women who haven't yet learned to have orgasm—who have driven their partners to distraction looking for the perfect touch and the perfect stroke. We've treated men with erection problems who have similarly burdened their partners with blame. They don't recognize that if they're getting *any* direct physical stimulation at all, they're getting as much as they need. After all, men have erections and ejaculations, and women experience lubrication and arousal, during sleep, with no physical stimulation whatsoever.

If you doubt this point, try an exercise. Ask your partner to stimulate you lightly and steadily and see what you can experience. You may be surprised how aroused you can let yourself become. Use the sensation that's there. It's more than enough to climb if you decide to let it be.

Similarly, when you find yourself face to face with a resistance, *concentrate on feeling*. If you're completely feeling, you won't be thinking about anything else. Your whole experience will be feeling. In a way your *thought* at that time is to *feel*. That's a strong, positive suggestion in itself, and by consistently willing it, you push resistance aside.

Your last experience with severe pain is a grim but vivid example of what we mean by "completely feeling." Maybe you smashed your thumb with a hammer. Maybe you stubbed your toe or cracked your shin. When the pain arrived it overwhelmed thinking. Afterward you probably had a thought or two about it. But before those thoughts came you were completely aware of pain and only of pain.

With ESO, you're working toward a state of complete, conscious awareness of pleasure—toward letting pleasure overwhelm you. The object of ESO training is to learn to achieve that state and then to stretch it out through time: to reach a point where you're not thinking *about* anything but simply, consciously, *experiencing*. Experiencing pleasure, where your entire experience is permeated with feeling and sensation.

Which isn't to advocate mindlessness. We don't. We think everyone needs a clear head to live decently and well. Your mind will be all the sharper later for having had the experience of an interlude of intense pleasure. You'll feel centered, relaxed, fulfilled, at peace. You'll probably also feel loved and loving.

Breathing

Breathing is a good way to work through resistance. Paying attention to breathing, especially deep, regular breathing from the diaphragm—with the stomach rising and falling rather than only the chest—helps, because it brings you back from thought to sensation, to your body. It helps because many people hold their breath when they're reaching for sexual arousal, tightening their muscles and reducing the oxygen supply to the brain.

Breathing also helps because the breathing reflex is complex and many bodily systems involved in sexual arousal are hooked into it. Breathing produces relaxation by changing the state of the body's autonomic nervous system. Relaxation reduces anxiety. And remember: there's anxiety behind each and every one of your resistances.

Visualization/Fantasy

Visualization can be a way of relaxing. Close your eyes while you're being pleasured and imagine you're somewhere else. On a Tahiti beach listening to the regular, smooth breaking of the waves, warming in the South Pacific sun. In a suite in a Swiss ski lodge on a fur rug before a crackling fire. In Paris between satin sheets in an elegant hotel. Choose someplace that makes you feel good and makes you feel peaceful and go there.

Sexual fantasy involves a variety of visualization techniques. Fantasy can chase resistances away. You imagine a desirable sexual experience with your partner or with someone else or you recall a pleasurable sexual experience you've had in the past. Some people fantasize more easily than others. Everyone can learn.

If you think you have difficulty fantasizing, try this exercise: start by closing your eyes and seeing yourself as you are right now, at this very moment, with your eyes closed, doing just what you are doing. Then experience your breathing. Notice your lungs filling and emptying and the sensation of your breath passing in and out your nose. Now, eyes closed, picture the objects in the room around you. Can you see them almost as clearly as if you had your eyes open? Picture yourself in the room among these objects. What are you wearing? Visualize your clothes.

Now change the scene. Visualize yourself on a soft, sandy beach, lying on powder-white sand in warm sun. Then picture someone with you on the beach.

Now switch to a sexual fantasy. Recall in detail a desirable sexual experience with your partner or with someone else. Or imagine a sexual experience that you would like to have at some future time. These memories and experiences may appear to you as snapshots, as movies, as fragmented and impressionistic images. They may involve feelings or words more than visual images.

Keep the fantasy in mind and build on it by adding new details. You can change the setting or add new experiences to real experiences you remember.

Knowing what other people fantasize about can help you learn to fantasize. Everyone has sexual fantasies some of the time. Here are common fantasies, listed in the order of their popularity:

(1) *Sex with your regular partner.* Pleasures you've enjoyed together in the past. Pleasures you'd like to enjoy but can't because you or your partner finds them unacceptable. Real experiences with imaginary embellishments. Feel free to invent any activities you think you would enjoy with your partner, however unlikely. They're your private fantasies and yours alone.

(2) *Sex with other opposite-sex partners.* Someone you have

met or known. Screen stars, sports heroes and heroines, your high school prom king or queen. Since this is fantasy, not reality, it's safe to pick anyone you want. Imagine where you are, what you're doing, what you say to each other. Visualize how your imagined partner looks and how touching and caressing feels. Decide what you would like to do. Mentally write an entire shared scene. You may be more comfortable with this fantasy if you also fantasize that your regular partner is having sex with someone else.

(3) *Sex with more than one partner.* A friend as well as your regular partner. A movie star, a famous man or woman. A man may fantasize a woman with full, sensuous lips stimulating him orally while his regular partner watches or joins in. A woman may imagine two men loving her physically at the same time, or a man and a woman. One may be a stranger and the other her regular partner.

(4) *Rape.* Fantasies of being taken sexually against your will. Women particularly enjoy this fantasy. It's perfectly acceptable. It has nothing to do with real rape, which is an ugly, violent act of criminal assault. Imagine being kidnapped, or someone breaking into your house. A stranger or someone you know takes you forcefully. Perhaps your regular partner is made to watch. You resist at first, then give in. You may be tied up and totally helpless but become sexually aroused along the way.

(5) *Sex with same-sex partners.* Most people fantasize occasionally about having sex with people of their own gender, although many strongly resist acknowledging these thoughts. If you aren't too threatened to explore this fantasy, picture in detail whom you would enjoy having sex with, what you would do, and where you would do it. Same-sex fantasies aren't an indication of homosexuality, conscious or unconscious. They're simply exercises in human imagination, a normal part of life.

(6) *Fantasies left over from childhood.* Vivid memories of fantasies and experiences may return to you from childhood

if you let them. Our first sexual experiences and feelings are often overwhelmingly powerful; you can tap some of that residual emotion by recalling them. They may be only fragmentary: a girl's hair brushing a boy's face; a glimpse of someone naked. You may have thought of playing doctor with another child, or of having sex with an adult. Recall those fantasies now.

Fantasies have great value in sex. They're private, so they affect no one else and depend on no one else, and they actually change body chemistry. They stimulate arousal; they can give you a head start on pleasure with your partner. The image comes before the reality and begins preparing the body for that reality.

If you find a fantasy arousing, continue that fantasy. If you find a fantasy neutral or negative, switch to another fantasy until you discover one that gives you pleasure.

Start with a fantasy that feels safe. Mentally write the scene. What time is it? Where are you? What does your partner (or partners) look like? What do both of you (or all of you) do? Begin dressed and enjoy undressing—even fantasies deserve time for foreplay! Don't rush your fantasy. Extending it will add pleasure and benefit arousal. If you are fantasizing about sex with someone other than your regular partner, choose someone with whom you feel comfortable. If the fantasy works, keep it going. If it doesn't work, change it.

Use fantasy in sexual situations. First fantasize alone while you self-stimulate. Then add fantasy while you're with your partner making love.

Some people fear they will act out their fantasies. Fantasies are almost always safe. Very few people ever act out fantasies they believe to be taboo.

Some people fear that fantasizing is dishonest. They believe they owe their partners one hundred percent of their physical and mental attention. They believe fantasizing is disloyal. They think that their partners would feel rejected and excluded if they knew. In fact, sharing fantasies often increases a partner's excitement. Partners should trust each other enough to share some fantasies. One way to test the water is to share a relatively safe fantasy and see what happens—a fantasy, for example, that involves only your partner and yourself, doing something together that you don't usually do. The sharing can develop from there.

Sharing fantasies can help enliven long-standing relationships when partners feel stuck sexually and bored. Fantasies add excitement and may also improve communication. Your partner may find renewed interest.

It's likely, in any case, that you and your partner both use sexual fantasies from time to time. Sometimes your partner's fantasies include you, sometimes not. Feel good about your fantasies—they'll enhance your shared pleasure.

Most of our clients find that regular fantasy helps them break through resistance. Replace resistance with fantasy to stimulate yourself to higher levels of arousal. That gives you more pleasure; it also gives your partner more pleasure.

Remember: fantasies are normal and healthy. You don't necessarily have to tell your partner about them. You're responsible for what you do in this world, not for what you think. By fantasizing during lovemaking you're helping yourself and your partner do what you both want to do, which is increase your mutual pleasure.

Suggestion

Suggestion is yet another way of relaxing, a way through resistance. If you see that your partner is struggling with resistance, you can offer positive suggestions. "You're getting more and more aroused." "You're really wonderful." "I love you." "Let yourself go." "That's nice." "Breathe—in and out." "Every time you breathe, you'll get higher." "Relax." "Trust me." "Yes, yes." "That's it." The right words, suggested quietly and with confidence, can help your partner through.

Monitoring Tension

We've said a lot already about Kegel exercises. We haven't talked about the more general question of pelvic muscle tension. Tension in the genital area strongly influences your level of sexual arousal. There's always pelvic muscle activity during sex, with tension either increasing or decreasing, so staying aware of that level of tension is always useful. Doing so won't be distracting. To the contrary, it focuses your attention on the area where you're receiving stimulation.

Then, when you encounter a resistance, you can add tension by contracting your P.C. muscle, holding it for six to eight seconds, relaxing it, and then pushing out. That shifts your attention from the resistance to a physical activity. It returns your attention to your genital area. It boosts arousal directly by stimulating the sexual tissues themselves.

Working your pelvic muscles to push through resistances and to build arousal has an important advantage over cognitive restructuring: it doesn't require thinking. You don't have to identify a resistance first and then decide how to deal with it. You only have to move from a resistance to a habitual muscular process. That automatically distracts you from the resistance. Each and every time a resistance appears you can start doing Kegel exercises or increase their intensity. You can always squeeze a little harder or a little longer.

Remember to breathe.

Changing Position

Finally, you can work through resistances by shifting your position and by subtle changes in movement. You can rotate your pelvis, arch your back, shift your legs, move to an entirely different position. That redirects your attention. Add a pillow. Remove a pillow. Turn to one side. Turn to the other side. Your partner can move along smoothly with you and can usually continue stimulating as you go.

The more time you spend at a point of resistance, carefully working through, the more progress you'll make. But stop before the experience becomes physically or psychologically painful. Otherwise you won't want to try it again.

IX

ESO: A HUMAN FUTURE

ESO and Health

Since the dim beginnings of human history, men have looked for miracle cures for the diseases and conditions that beset them. They've sought from one continent to the next, from one discipline to the next, from one fad to the next, for fountains of youth and magic diets and miracle cures, despite their general failure.

It's just possible that regularly experienced ESO could supply some of the missing magic. We've seen improvement, often dramatic improvement, in an astounding variety of symptoms in people who have regularly practiced ESO. These are some of the symptoms and problems that ESO seems to have improved and in some cases eliminated:

Physical symptoms:
headaches (migraine, tension, allergic)
chronic pain (back, neck, pelvis)
menstrual pain syndrome

    arthritic pain
    stomach and gastrointestinal complaints
    prostatitis
    high blood pressure
    asthma and bronchitis
    skin eruptions (dermatitis and psoriasis)
Emotional problems:
    depression, "low energy," constant fatigue
    anxiety
    alcoholism and some drug dependencies
    insomnia
    marital conflict
    explosive anger

This list is preliminary. We suspect that it's incomplete and will expand as we gain experience in the effects on men and women of ESO practiced over longer periods of time.

Why these broad and profound effects? It's really not that surprising. The sexual response system is linked to many different bodily systems: the nervous system, both central—brain—and autonomic—self-regulating; the circulatory system and the heart; the musculature; the system of hormone production; the gastrointestinal system. Sex also involves all the body's organs. Sexual responsiveness is every human being's birthright, an intrinsically natural, healthy function. ESO gives the body a vigorous workout, restoring natural balance.

It's at least as effective as regular exercise—jogging, for example. Jogging feels like too much work at first. But after you practice, after it becomes a habit, it's easy, fun, and automatic. Regular joggers find that when they stop jogging, even for only a few days, they feel the loss mentally and physically. This acclimation is also true of ESO.

The beneficial health effects of regular exercise are well documented. Exercise operates to restore the balanced functioning of a variety of bodily systems. Regular ESO appears to be at least as effective as regular exercise. In fact, because ESO reaches into the depths of emotional life as mere exercise can never do, it's far more influential on health and happiness. Regular ESO—ideally, daily ESO—is the strongest as well as the safest, and certainly the most pleasurable, medicine we know. Unlike other treatments or medications available, ESO is *totally safe*. There are *no* reported bad side effects.

Sex and Aging

Age is no barrier to sex. It's no barrier either to ESO. None of us uses more than a small fraction of his sexual potential. By learning to use more, men and women of any age can increase their response, often beyond the levels they achieved when they were younger.

One of our favorite clients is a seventy-year-old former professional actor. Mike came to see us one day because, as he said, "It just hangs limp." He had erection problems.

Mike had all but given up sex. We assigned him daily self-stimulation exercise. We coached him that better functioning was possible. He began to trust us. He began dating. He's discovered now that he can have three or four separate ejaculations a day, which is more than he'd enjoyed for thirty years.

Mike didn't stop there. He learned ESO. He's taught it to a variety of partners. Now he's one of the most popular widowers in town. He's a very happy man.

We've seen many couples and individuals who have increased their sexual abilities to high levels, more than compensating for their natural decline with aging. Regular self-stimulation for fifteen minutes or more at a time is crucial to that increase. So are Kegel exercises. The first and most important requirement is giving sex time and priority in your life.

Studies show that people who have frequent sexual activity in their younger years have sex much more frequently in their older years than do people whose sexual activities have been limited all along. The best guarantee of a good sex life in your later years is making sure you have a good sex life in your earlier years. But even if your sexual activities have been limited, you can usually improve significantly by following the guidelines in this book. Every activity and experience we've discussed here should be available to you, regardless of your age. It's good for your health. It's good for life.

Share Your Experiences

We spend about twenty percent of our time at our center in Palo Alto practicing sex therapy and training clients in ESO. Their progress especially interests and delights us. Changes usually come faster and more dramatically than in any other treatment program. Even clients who arrive severely depressed about the level of their sexual functioning usually leave happier than they ever thought possible.

Discovering, by experience, that vastly more pleasure is possible than you imagined, even in fantasy, always has a powerful impact. When the intensity of your sexual responses and the practiced excellence of your sexual skills exceed anything you have heard or read or seen, your personality and your values change. You gain self-confidence. You discover optimism. You're happy.

We've seen these changes, and the many others that we've discussed in this book, in clients who have learned ESO. But there is much more to learn about the physical and mental conditions that characterize ESO. We've concentrated first on developing ESO techniques and devising ways to teach them because scientific studies can't be done without a trained population to work with. As we mentioned earlier, we have begun one such study: preliminary work demonstrating what appear to be characteristic changes in brainwave patterns in both men and women during ESO. We are also looking at how these brainwave changes correlate with vaginal and rectal contractions, heart rate, blood pressure, and other physical measures.

We invite and eagerly await the completion of further studies which identify more precisely the changes in male and female physiology during and after ESO. Suggestive scientific data are already filtering in. For example, it has been reported that in a group of arthritics, those who experienced orgasm felt significant pain relief for up to half an hour. That report suggests that orgasm may very well increase the level of endorphins in the human brain (endorphins are recently discovered natural opiate-like substances produced in the brain that are sixty times more potent than morphine and influence mood and mental functioning). If a ten-second orgasm can increase endorphin levels enough to reduce arthritic pain for half an hour, what might be the effect on pain of an hour of ESO?

Equally as important as laboratory research are the candid reports of men and women who explore this mostly uncharted area of sexual functioning on their own.

We invite and encourage you to write to us about your personal experiences as you move toward, learn, or regularly practice ESO.

Please address your letters to The Institute for the Study of ESO, Box 6050, Stanford, CA 94305.

The following questionnaire asks some of the questions to which we're seeking answers. You can write directly on the page and mail the pages in. Or you can copy the pages and answer on the copy. Please feel free to attach additional pages to add to or clarify your answers. You don't need to include your name and address with the questionnaire. The answers you give will help us prepare future reports.

REPLY QUESTIONNAIRE

1. Your age _____ Marital status _____
   City and state of residence _____
   Male or female _____

2. Have you seen any change in the length or type of your orgasms? Yes _____ No _____
   Please comment: _____
   _____
   _____
   _____

3. Average number of times per month you experience
   Stage I (single orgasm) _____
   Stage II (multiple orgasm) _____
   Stage III ESO (Phase I, Reaching) _____
                 (Phase II, Orgasmic track) _____

4. Average maximum length of time you experience ESO
   _____ seconds/minutes   (circle one)

5. How long did it take you to learn ESO?
   _____ weeks/months   (circle one)

6. If you have been regularly experiencing ESO, have you noticed any positive effects that you can attribute to ESO on your (circle areas that apply)
   (a) physical health
   (b) emotional or mental state
   (c) relationship with your sexual partner or partners
   (d) other relationships—family, friends, work?

7. Have you or your partner located a vaginal internal trigger area (G spot)?
   Yes / No / Does not apply   (circle one)

8. Does stimulation of this internal trigger area play an important part in your or your partner's best orgasms?
   Yes / No   (circle one)

9. Have you or your partner located the prostate area, either through the external prostate spot or by internal stimulation?

Yes / No / Does not apply   (circle one)

10. Does stimulation of this area play an important part in your or your partner's best orgasms?

Yes / No / Does not apply   (circle one)

11. For women only:

(a) If you are aware of contractions, what type do you *usually* experience during orgasms?

Squeeze / Push-out / Alternating squeeze and push-out / Combined squeeze and push-out   (circle those that apply)

(b) Which type of contraction do you usually experience with your *best* orgasms?

Squeeze / Push-out / Alternating squeeze and push-out / Combined squeeze and push-out   (circle one)

12. For men only:

(a) How much clear fluid do you or your partner notice you secrete *prior to ejaculation*? Number of drops/teaspoons   (circle one) _____

(b) Have you noticed any increase in the size of your penis when it is fully erect?

Yes / No   (circle one)

(c) If your answer to (b) is yes, how much increase?

Length _____ inch(es)

Diameter _____ inch(es)

We would also like to hear from men and women who wanted to extend their orgasmic pleasure, or started to extend their orgasmic pleasure, but whose resistances, fears, or conflicts interfered. A discussion of your experience and your comments on it would greatly help us with our work. Everyone who responds can take satisfaction in the knowledge that the information you send us will specifically benefit research that will increase the health and happiness of many other men and women. We will of course protect the confidentiality of your communications in any reports we may prepare.

Any reader who wishes to be included on the mailing list of The Institute for the Study of ESO may send in his or her name and address to the Institute at Box 6050, Stanford, CA 94305 USA.

A Final Word

As with all challenging journeys, not everyone who starts out to learn ESO will arrive there. Some of you will decide you don't want to begin the trip. That's fine. No one should travel who isn't intrigued by newness, adventure, and the excitement of uncertainty. Even if you decide not to attempt any of the training programs described in this book, simply having read it may begin to improve your sexual experience in subtle ways.

Others may give up and turn back before reaching ESO. We encourage you to talk over your fears and resistances with your partner. Every journey faces the traveler with periods of discouragement and disillusionment. *Keep going!* If you share your doubts with your partner, he or she may help you find the incentive you need to continue. Even the process of sharing is likely itself to improve your relationship. When your partner is the one discouraged, your encouragement may be the critical factor that supplies a reason to go on. Remember as well that getting there is half the fun, and even when you arrive, you won't have come to an end. There's always more pleasure to discover in lovemaking, we're delighted to say.

If you have just read through this book for the first time, congratulations on your willingness to come this far in developing your sexual potential. We encourage you now to begin to practice what you've learned.

Sexual energy may be like nuclear energy, a vastly powerful force hidden in history until it was accidentally discovered and tapped. If it is, it is energy entirely on the side of life. Your natural resistances will assure that you will unfold your sexual potential only gradually and safely.

What we are learning, studying, and teaching is a new *human* technology for increasing *human* pleasure. The important human experience of sexual intimacy no longer has to be left to accidents of self-discovery and the vagaries of ancient prescription. The blind no longer have to lead the blind. The new sexual technology seeks to understand sexual responses and find ways to make them better under a variety of conditions from handicapped to optimum. Some will not be surprised, and others will be relieved, to hear that the highest forms of sexual response seem to occur between two people who love and trust each other.

In all that we've said here and in all that you do, remember to enjoy yourself. Don't be too programmatic. Don't turn pleasure into work. Goals help, in sex as elsewhere, but choose pleasure first when you're making love. That's what this book is: a program for pleasure—fluid, fluent, and deeply human.

Enjoy your journey. We certainly are!

It becomes a dance.

Achieving ESO: A Checklist

1. Assume that ESO is possible.
2. Acknowledge that you want and deserve more sexual pleasure.
3. Decide to train for ESO.
4. Have a partner who shares equally in wanting to experience ESO.
5. Learn the procedures and techniques of ESO.
6. Practice ESO training for two to four hours a week.
7. Talk frequently with your partner about your positive and negative sexual feelings.
8. Find courage to continue training despite possible setbacks along the way.

APPENDIX: SOLVING PROBLEMS

WE'VE INCLUDED this section in our book because some levels of sexual functioning need to be changed before ESO becomes possible. We won't go into as much detail here as we did in previous chapters. Many men and women will be able to work through their problems with the information we supply here. Some won't. For them we advise counseling with competent sex therapists.

Many people with sexual problems will find it helpful to practice the exercises and procedures described in Chapters III and IV. Some people with problems will find that following the ESO training program can be useful to improve their functioning, without making extending orgasm a goal. But there's much to learn as well in this appendix. We strongly recommend that everyone read it through at least once, regardless of your level of sexual functioning and your degree of sexual sophistication.

Sexual Problems

Defining Sexual Problems

You have a sexual problem if there's a significant gap between what you expect your experience should be and what it actually is.

That's a much more accurate description than the ugly labels that self-appointed authorities sometimes still use, labels like *frigid, impotent, incompetent.* Sexual functioning isn't fitted to some universal standard. The range is enormous. So is the potential, as we've seen. No one—not even men and women trained in ESO—achieves full sexual potential. In that sense we all have sexual problems.

The only person who can validly identify a problem area in your sexual functioning is you. A man might define himself as an early ejaculator if he ejaculates sooner than he and his partner wish and doesn't know how to delay orgasm. A woman might define herself as situationally nonorgasmic if she can stimulate herself to orgasm but doesn't know how to have orgasm with her partner during intercourse and wants to.

Medical Problems

Not all sexual problems are psychological. Some are medical and physical. Diabetes can cause sexual problems. So can prostate surgery, chronic infections, torn ligaments, excessive alcohol, chronic illness, chronic pain, and many physical difficulties. A variety of medications can interfere, particularly tranquilizers and drugs for high blood pressure. If you suspect your problem is medical, visit a physician for a thorough examination.

Even if you have a physical condition that can affect you sexually, deliberate effort to improve your sexual functioning—such as by following the exercises and programs described in this book—can improve your sexual experience. There are very few people, even with severe medical disabilities such as diabetes or paraplegia, who cannot learn to have better-quality sex than they now think possible. Unfortunately, their doubts are often reinforced by their doctors, families, and friends. Our advice: don't believe prophets of sexual doom. Give pleasure a try.

Anxiety

Most sexual problems arise from lack of knowledge, emotional concerns, or lack of experience. Most can be corrected, then, with information and practice.

Anxiety is the root cause of sexual difficulties. It shows up as fear, tension, stress, and resistance. That's why we've emphasized relaxation techniques throughout this book. We'll refer to those techniques again here as we discuss what to do about problems.

Most problems can be solved—most gaps can be closed— using basically the same skills as those you develop for ESO. So what you learn here can be carried forward directly into that training. You'll even have the advantage of many people, because you'll already have learned how to work through tough problems of resistance.

Traumatic Early Experience

Some sexual problems can be worked through best in long-term therapy—psychotherapy or psychoanalysis. These are usually problems that go back to childhood: a background of severe punishment for sexual behavior; severe conflict about sexual behavior; traumatic incest; other traumatic early sexual experiences. These experiences can produce anxiety that's too deep-seated to give way to the self-training methods we discuss here. If you find yourself unable to make progress by these methods, you may want to work with a competent psychiatrist or psychologist. But most people can greatly improve their sexual skills without long-term therapy.

Male problems

Since women go first in ESO training, we'll talk about gentlemen first here: erection problems, then problems with timing ejaculation.

Erection problems come in two degrees of severity: the primary problem of the man who has *never* been able to maintain an erection in intercourse and, less severe, the secondary problem of the man who *sometimes* can't maintain an erection in intercourse.

Primary Erection Problems

A man with a primary erection problem has *never* been able to sustain an erection for intercourse with any partner. Erections are usually possible with masturbation and sometimes with manual or oral stimulation by a partner. Often primary erection problems originate in deep-seated emotional conflicts about sex or about women. Although the methods for improving secondary erection problems described below are frequently helpful, men who experience primary erection problems may benefit from longer-term psychotherapy.

Secondary Erection Problems

More commonly, men who complain of erection difficulties have functioned relatively well at some time in the past. About fifteen percent of the men in this category are likely to have a problem with their health.

At least once a week, do you find yourself moderately to fully erect when you awaken from sleep at night or in the morning? If you think not, or don't know, try the postage-stamp test. Stick together a ring of postage stamps around your penis when you go to bed. If the ring is broken open in the morning, you probably had an erection during sleep. If the stamp ring is intact, you probably didn't. Can you get an erection when you self-stimulate? If the answer to both these questions is no, then you should certainly consult a medical doctor. If the answer to both these questions is yes, then the chances are good that the problem is psychological.

No male, throughout his entire life, maintains an erection during intercourse one hundred percent of the time. The erection mechanism isn't that reliable. Sex therapists usually call it a problem if a patient has difficulty maintaining an erection during intercourse more than twenty-five percent of the time. That's one out of four. If your difficulty is less frequent than that, you're probably normal. The majority of men function more or less the same. Your problem can be dealt with by learning to overcome resistance and to take in more pleasure. ESO training is a good way to do both.

But twenty-five percent is only a general rule of thumb. A patient of ours who's a rock star showed us how subjective these rules can be. He came to us complaining of erection problems. When we sat down and charted the difficulty, it averaged out at about twenty percent. We didn't consider twenty percent a problem, but in his world that percentage was catastrophic. His professional image is highly sexual. His female partners expected him to show them the best night of their lives. They expected one hundred twenty percent function. When he couldn't produce and maintain an erection, he felt humiliated.

We asked him to list the times he could and the times he couldn't. A pattern emerged that he hadn't noticed: he had trouble with erection when he'd been using drugs and alcohol. He agreed then not to put himself into sexual situations when he had recently used alcohol or drugs. That helped. With relaxation training he was soon back to his high-average normal.

Our first point, then, is simply reassurance: no one maintains erection successfully all the time. Fatigue, tension, stress, anxiety, distraction, and chemicals all can intervene.

Your partner needs to recognize that her pleasure is not totally dependent on your erection. You can stimulate her by other means. One of the advantages of ESO training is that it relieves you of performance pressure. If you feel you have secondary erection problems, go ahead and get started with ESO training.

A ban on intercourse can be extremely helpful. Ideally you'll want your partner's cooperation. Otherwise she may begin to wonder why you've lost interest.

We'd suggest you agree with your partner not to have intercourse for at least six sexual encounters—somewhere in the vicinity of a month. You can find pleasure, and give your partner pleasure, any other way you care to, but during that time you won't have intercourse. This simple agreement is the single most useful method we know of for dealing with erection problems.

If you don't have a regular sexual partner, or if your sexual partner can't be included in your decision, you can decide unilaterally to ban intercourse. If you do, you should give your partner more attention in other ways sexually so that she won't miss intercourse as much and won't put so much pressure on you to have intercourse. This unilateral ban isn't as desirable as a ban with your partner's agreement, but it's better than none at all.

With a ban on intercourse you'll probably notice that your erections return. You shouldn't expect them to return all at once. But eventually, with other sexual stimulation, they will. It's important then that you don't try immediately to use your erection for intercourse.

Along with an intercourse ban you should follow the self-stimulation program in Chapter III, "Developing Skills." Don't try to achieve advanced levels of extended arousal yet. Concentrate on achieving and sustaining an erection by self-stimulation for fifteen minutes and then go on to ejaculation.

The Sensory Focus exercise on p. 76 is very useful to help reduce performance anxiety in men who have trouble achieving and sustaining erection. Go through all four steps at least four different times. Then you may concentrate on steps three and four, with ejaculation allowed as a conclusion.

When you are able to achieve reliable erection during Sensory Focus, step three, you and your partner have a choice. You may proceed to intercourse at the end of this period of manual stimulation by your partner, or you may go on with ESO training. Refer to the discussion on p. 78, "Are You Ready for ESO?" to guide you in determining your readiness to go on with ESO training. You may then want to resume intercourse when you are able to experience extended orgasms lasting twice as long as those you experienced before training. Men who learn to experience Phase I ESO for several minutes, several times a week, are likely to have fewer problems with erections during intercourse.

Erection problems often occur because a man believes he should automatically experience an erection whenever he's in a sexual situation. Women often believe that too.

It's a myth. Most men need their penises directly stimulated for erection. The need increases with age. A partner is the best source of that stimulation, so you should continue self-stimulation training through the stages when your partner watches you to learn how and then takes over the process.

You are responsible for arranging enough stimulation. You have to make sure you give yourself enough or your partner gives you enough. Then, even if you don't begin a sexual encounter with an erection, you can produce an erection with self-stimulation. If you've done that in front of your partner in training, then you won't be embarrassed to do it again when it's needed. And yes, it's okay, many men stimulate themselves in order to achieve a working level of arousal. It's more fun if your partner does it for you, but not all women are willing to agree. It's your penis, your pleasure, and ultimately your responsibility.

Soft Penis Intercourse can be a useful exercise for erection problems. Both partners experience pleasure from penile stimulation that isn't dependent on erection. It's also a pleasurable variation for any couple to use near the beginning of a sexual encounter, because it establishes sexual intimacy without rushing sexual performance.

The woman lies on her back with her right leg tented over the man's hips. The man lies at a forty-five degree angle to her body on his left side, facing her. He holds his penis in his right hand and rubs the glans up, down, and around the woman's clitoris. Both areas, penis and vulva, should be well lubricated. (See illustration number 12.)

The man should concentrate on stimulating his glans, focusing his attention on the pleasurable sensations he receives from rubbing it against his partner's genitals. The woman should allow herself to enjoy the clitoral stimulation she's receiving without thinking ahead to what she hopes or anticipates should happen—to her arousal or to his.

If you, the man, happen to develop an erection during this exercise, don't be concerned. Continue the stimulation. If you sustain an erection for five minutes or more, you may partly insert yourself—no more than one inch—into your

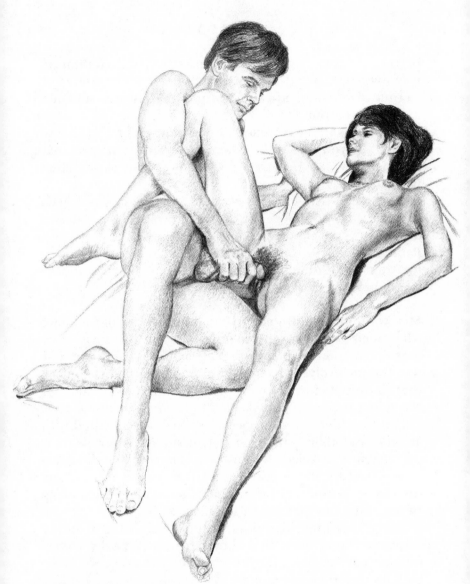

Positions for Intercourse

(12) Soft-Penis Intercourse
Training and foreplay exercise. Man rhythmically rubs soft penis against woman's vaginal opening and clitoris. As penis hardens, man rhythmically inserts and withdraws.

partner's vagina. If you do partly insert yourself, continue to use your right hand to move your penis from inside the vagina to outside, up and around the clitoris—in, out, around and around.

After five minutes or more of partial insertion and clitoral teasing, if you are still sustaining an erection, you may gradually increase penetration while decreasing clitoral stimulation.

Do this exercise at least five times a week for at least fifteen minutes each session, even if you or your partner resists doing it, even if it bores you. Don't expect an erection. Soft Penis Intercourse is a training exercise. Boxers jump rope for training to develop their reflexes and stamina, not because they expect to jump rope in the ring.

Men with erection problems should make a list of the times when their penises rise to the occasion and the times when they don't. You may identify a pattern. The pattern the rock star found involved drugs and alcohol. He hadn't noticed that pattern before. Alcohol is a very common cause of erection problems. The classic alcohol-related disability is failing to achieve erection because you're anesthetized with alcohol and then panicking and assuming your penis is permanently disabled. Performance anxiety after that sustains a self-fulfilling prophecy. Up to two drinks in any three-hour period can help rather than hinder sexual experience, but more than that may interfere.

There are other difficulties you might discover by listing occasions. Some men find they have no difficulty with a familiar partner but difficulty with a new partner. For other men it's the other way around.

Especially with a familiar partner, you can solve your problem by finding ways to make sex feel new, different, and more exciting. Change the time, change the setting, change the position. One certain new adventure that you and your partner might arrange for yourselves is agreement to train for ESO.

You need to learn how to reduce anxiety. We've discussed methods in Chapter VIII, "Overcoming Resistances." Learn to relax. Work on cognitive restructuring. Practice breathing exercises. Work on visualization. Have your partner use positive suggestion. All those techniques will help.

Just as you're responsible for arranging enough stimulation, so also you're responsible for deciding when you feel up to lovemaking. Don't have sex just because you think you ought to. If you're feeling pressed, if you have a deadline the next morning, you should recognize that you're in conflict and aren't likely to give pleasure your full attention. It's great to agree never to say no to sex, but if you have an erection problem, you're not ready yet for that agreement.

Men have more trouble saying no than women do. It's important to say no in a way that won't hurt your partner's feelings. Be honest. Don't tell her you have a headache. Admit you have a deadline to meet the following day and you're preoccupied. Offer an alternative: "Can we agree to make love tomorrow night instead? Because then I'll be more attentive."

This approach applies as well to situations that provoke anxiety. You're not required to make love where you're uncomfortable. Some years ago we worked with an adventurous woman married to a conservative man. Melanie would propose making love in the woods in broad daylight or in a car parked on a city street and Arthur would be appalled. We suggested compromise. They both moved a little toward the middle. Now they make love in the woods at night or parked on a back-country road. Arthur's working toward becoming more adventurous because Melanie likes it and he's finding he likes a touch of it too.

Drugs other than alcohol can also cause problems. We don't mean only illegal drugs. We're often surprised to find clients taking several prescribed medications without realizing that they may affect sexual functioning. Tranquilizers and sleeping pills are serious offenders. So are drugs for high blood pressure. If you're taking medication and have erection problems, you should discuss that medication with your doctor. Doctors are often reluctant to tell you in advance about possible sexual side effects of the medications they prescribe, because the information itself can trigger problems in anxious patients.

If you use marijuana, don't use too much too frequently. Used recreationally, no more than once a week, it can be helpful, creating some slowing of the time sense, loosening inhibitions, and allowing you to focus more on feelings than on thoughts. On the other hand some people have bad reactions—more anxiety and sometimes paranoia. And reliable research has shown that chronic—daily—marijuana use decreases testosterone levels and thus decreases libido.

In general we favor natural pleasures over chemical pleasures. Your body produces hormones and other substances when it's sexually stimulated that enhance pleasure and increase libido—endorphins, androgens. The best way to maintain healthy hormone levels is to enjoy frequent sex.

If, however, you have erection problems and haven't had your testosterone level checked, you might discuss that measurement with your doctor. If he finds a low testosterone level, he may want to prescribe pills or, better, injections. Bimonthly testosterone injections for about two months can sometimes help erection problems. Work on sexual skills during those two months. You may increase your testosterone production naturally then and won't need further supplement.

Early Ejaculation

Early ejaculation is a timing problem. You ejaculate before you want to or before your partner wants you to. In sports we admire quick reflexes. In bed they can cause difficulties. But it's not farfetched, in the context of ESO, to say that all men are early ejaculators. Very few of us can make love for three hours at a stretch.

It's possible to learn. You only have to want to. You'll be able to give your partner more pleasure in lovemaking if you can last longer. That's the traditional rationale. It's true and valid. But less often emphasized is another reason for learning to delay ejaculation, equally valid and perhaps even more in your interest: you'll give yourself more pleasure too. Go back to p. 123 and look at the graph of male orgasmic responses. It demonstrates that the longer your erection can last, the higher your arousal and the more total pleasure you'll have.

In Chapter IV, "Getting Together," we discuss foreplay. A formal exercise in foreplay is Sensory Focus, p. 76, which is a good way to begin dealing with early ejaculation problems. Many men ejaculate sooner than they and their partners would like because they focus all their attention on their genitals. They fail to realize that their entire bodies are available for sexual stimulation. To the degree that you can allow your whole body to participate in lovemaking, you'll be able to take in more pleasure longer without tripping the ejaculation reflex.

Sensory Focus involves your partner. She needs actively to caress you. Some women don't think that's their job. They see themselves as simply a receptacle, or they look out for their own orgasm and expect a man to do the same. Don't accept those terms. If your partner wants you to last longer, she should be willing to help you learn how.

After Sensory Focus, you and your partner can go on to ejaculation-control training. You lie on your back, knees flexed or extended, and your partner sits or kneels between your legs. She lubricates your penis and scrotum and begins stimulating your penis—stroking it—until you approach orgasm. She concentrates on learning the signs of approaching orgasm: thrusting hips, jerky body movements, lifting of the testicles upward against the body, pulsing of the penis itself.

You can help her by quickly withdrawing your pelvis as a signal or by telling her where you are: "I'm getting close." "Stop." But eventually she needs to learn to know without being told.

When you're close to orgasm, your partner simply stops stimulating you—stops stroking, or even takes her hands away for a few seconds, up to a full minute. Your level of arousal will decline. When it has declined to where you feel in control, she starts stimulating again. She might stop and start at least six times in fifteen minutes.

If you go over to orgasm and ejaculation, open your mind and body. Relax, flowing into the ejaculation experience. Afterward discuss with your partner what happened and how both of you can achieve better control next time. The exercise in semen withholding on p. 56 can help you achieve better control of ejaculation. It's the opposite of letting go and relaxing.

Another control technique your partner can learn is the scrotal pull, which is discussed on p. 112 in Chapter VI, "ESO: Giving a Man Pleasure." As you may have noticed by now, early ejaculation-control training is similar to ESO training. The one leads directly to the other.

Practice ejaculatory control by the Sensory Focus Steps III and IV and stop-start methods at least twice a week until you achieve control. When you can last thirty minutes with your partner stimulating you, you may be ready to go on to ESO training.

Manual stimulation is different from vaginal. A man might have no problem with manual stimulation but ejaculate as soon as he enters his partner's vagina. To desensitize yourself to intercourse, here's a ten-step training program you can follow. It incorporates as steps three and four the stop-start method we just discussed. Stop whenever you feel ejaculation is near and then start again.

Ten-Step Training Program
for Early Ejaculators

(1) Stimulate yourself with a dry hand until you can last for thirty minutes.

(2) Stimulate yourself with a lubricated hand until you can last for thirty minutes.

(3) Have your partner stimulate you with dry hands until you can last for thirty minutes.

(4) Have your partner stimulate you with lubricated hands until you can last for thirty minutes.

(5) Lie on your back. Have your partner kneel facing you, astride. Keep your penis in her vagina, moving only enough to maintain erection, until you can last for thirty minutes.

(6) Lie on your back. Have your partner kneel facing you, astride. With your penis inside her, she thrusts gently, stopping when necessary for control, until you can last for thirty minutes.

(7) Lie on your back. Have your partner kneel facing you, astride. With your penis inside her, you thrust gently, stopping when necessary for control, until you can last for thirty minutes.

(8) Lie on your back. Have your partner kneel facing you, astride. With your penis inside her, both of you thrust, stopping when necessary for control, until you can last for thirty minutes.

(9) Make love lying on your sides until you can last for thirty minutes.

(10) Make love in the missionary position for thirty minutes.

Use this program at least twice a week for six months. Complete ejaculatory control may require two to six months of training. You'll regress sometimes. That's normal and nothing to worry about. Just go back to Sensory Focus and stop-start. You may also find yourself experiencing occasional problems maintaining your erection. That's normal too. Look over the section entitled "Secondary Erection Problems," p. 173, for guidance then.

You'll also want to learn to relax. Reread Chapter VIII, "Overcoming Resistances," for instruction.

Do Kegel exercises faithfully. They're an excellent way to control ejaculation.

If you're clenching your pelvic muscles when climbing to arousal, then quickly push out and stop breathing for a moment to control the urge to ejaculate. If you're pushing out to climb to arousal, then momentarily clench your pelvic muscles as tightly as you can and hold your breath to control the urge to ejaculate. These controls are much easier if you've regularly practiced Kegel exercises.

Delayed Ejaculation

Delayed ejaculation is a relatively less common problem. If you often have vaginal intercourse with an erection for thirty minutes or more but then are unable to ejaculate vaginally even if you want to, you may have a problem with delayed ejaculation. Delayed ejaculators can usually ejaculate in other situations—when self-stimulating, for example.

The problem is almost always caused by a severe resistance to allowing semen to enter the vagina, and it's often best dealt with in psychotherapy. Relaxation techniques can help. So can self-stimulation exercises fitted to intercourse.

Those work this way: you stimulate yourself almost to the point of ejaculation and then insert your penis into your partner's vagina at the final moment to finish. When you can ejaculate inside the vagina that way, then at later sessions of lovemaking, insert yourself at earlier and earlier stages before ejaculation. After a month or more, you may find you won't need to stimulate yourself at all prior to intercourse, except possibly to achieve an erection.

Another approach to delayed ejaculation is by way of Sensory Focus (p. 76) and partner stimulation. Your partner should do Sensory Focus with you. Follow the self-stimulation and partner-stimulation training program we describe in Chapter III, "Developing Skills." When your partner has learned how you like to be pleasured, she should practice stimulating you by hand to orgasm. Then, at a later session, she should take you up to the point where you're ready to ejaculate and then insert your penis into her vagina with you on your back and her kneeling facing you, astride. At successive sessions she should insert you progressively earlier. She can also help by doing rhythmic push-outs to increase penile stimulation.

Female Problems

Women experience two basic kinds of sexual difficulties: problems with orgasm and painful intercourse. Problems with orgasm divide between those women who have never had orgasm and those who have it only in some situations but not in others.

Preorgasmia

If you have never learned to have orgasm, either with a partner or alone, by any means, you're preorgasmic. Preorgasmia is the easiest of all female sexual problems to correct. More than ninety percent of preorgasmic women can learn to have orgasm through a directed program.

The key is self-stimulation. To learn to have orgasm you need to be willing to practice regular self-stimulation. All the advantages of sexual pleasure, for yourself and for your partner, follow from that decision.

You should practice relaxation techniques and anxiety reduction. See Chapter VIII, "Overcoming Resistances," for guidance.

You need to learn Kegel exercises and to do them faithfully, as discussed on p. 91.

You can learn to have orgasm, and then to have orgasm during intercourse, by following a ten-step program. Practice each step until you complete it successfully before going on to the next step.

Do these exercises every day.

Ten-Step Training Program for Preorgasmic Women

(1) Stand nude in front of a full-length mirror. Look at your body as if you were another person. Be neutral, not critical. Assess yourself. Find your good points. Very few women ever take time to look at their bodies. See if you can agree to appreciate your body as it is, as worthy of pleasure.

Look over your genitals. Examine them. Learn where things are.

(2) In a comfortable, private place, such as lying alone in bed, touch yourself for pleasure, not sexual arousal. Include your genitals in your touching, but with no expectation of arousal. Enjoy touching and being touched. Notice what feels good.

(3) In a comfortable, private place touch yourself for arousal. With your eyes and your hands, explore your body and your genitals to discover the areas that are most sexually sensitive. Touch your scalp, your neck, your shoulders. Touch your nipples to see what feels good. Does firmness feel best? Does rolling your nipples between thumb and forefinger feel best? Touch your belly. Touch the insides of your thighs, your labia, your clitoris. Learn what feels good so that later you can teach your partner. He won't know what you like unless you teach him. You can't teach him if you don't know yourself.

(4) In a comfortable, private place stimulate yourself for arousal (without seeking orgasm) in the areas you identified in step three as sexually sensitive. Use a lubricant when you stimulate your genitals (see "Lubrication," p. 204).

(5) Stimulate yourself more intensely over a longer period of time, at least thirty minutes or more every day. Allow orgasm to happen naturally. If, after two weeks of daily stimulation, you haven't had orgasm, go on to step six.

(6) Using a vibrator, stimulate yourself in turn on each of the sensitive areas you've identified, working your way to your genitals. (See "Vibrators," p. 212.) Include clitoral stimulation and bring yourself to orgasm. If one type of vibrator doesn't seem to work for you, try another kind. If the vibrator feels too intense, put a towel between it and your genitals. Or use water from a tub faucet or flexible shower hose. A flexible shower hose with the head removed is a superb tool for sensual pleasure. Relax in the bathtub and adjust a warm soft flow from the hose. Direct the flow all over your genitals, then focus the flow on your clitoris for exquisite sensations. Start with a gentle flow and later experiment with greater pressure.

If, after two or three weeks of daily exercises, you are unable to have orgasm using a vibrator, consult a sex therapist or a training group. Many women's organizations offer group counseling for preorgasmia. That's the least expensive form of treatment, and it gets results. Call around.

When you achieve orgasm with a vibrator (congratulations!), see if you can then learn to have orgasm without a vibrator. Use the vibrator to get close to the point of orgasm. Then switch to your hand. When you can take over orgasm with your hand, stop using the vibrator a little earlier each week. Eventually you should be able to give yourself orgasm using your hands alone.

(7) Stimulate yourself to orgasm with your partner observing.

(8) Allow your partner to stimulate you to orgasm as you demonstrated in step seven.

(9) During intercourse allow your partner to stimulate you to orgasm as he learned in step eight. The best position for this exercise is the rear-entry position with both of you kneeling (see illustration number 8) or with the man standing beside the bed. He can reach around in this position to stimulate your clitoris with his hands.

(10) Stimulate yourself to orgasm during intercourse.

Orgasm Sometimes, but Not with Intercourse

Women who have orgasm with self-stimulation or partner stimulation but not with intercourse need first to consider how assertive they are. They are often women who have been taught to believe that the man's pleasure always comes first. One practical problem with that conviction is that when a woman encourages a man to ejaculate before she's had orgasm, she no longer has an erect penis available to work with.

First of all, then, be sure you're taking what you need. You may want to extend the time you spend in foreplay and intercourse. You may want to make sure the conditions of lovemaking suit you. (See Chapter II, "Creating the Conditions for Pleasure," p. 7.) You may want to choose a more arousing position for lovemaking. Subservience doesn't work in bed. Your needs are just as important as your partner's.

Another approach is to assign yourself the pleasure of having orgasm in ways different from what is usual for you. Find a different position or make subtle changes in the angles and movements within positions you are already using. If you haven't been using a vibrator with intercourse, try it. If you've been making love only in bed, make love somewhere else. Deliberately alter some habitual patterns. Focus on the pleasurable sensations you *do* feel during intercourse rather than on the ones you *think* you should be feeling. This will encourage sensations to grow.

ESO training is an excellent way to deal with this problem. Your ability to experience orgasm with manual vaginal stimulation is enhanced. If you are able to experience an orgasm of several minutes or more by manual stimulation, your vagina will become heavily engorged with blood and pleasurably sensitive. It's much easier then to continue the orgasmic experience with a thrusting penis.

Situational Nonorgasmia

If you've had orgasm in the past, but are presently unable to have orgasm by any means at all, this is your category. Situational nonorgasmia usually signals a change in your health, your relationship, or your attitude.

Has your physical condition changed? Do you have an infection? Have you started to have a problem with drugs or alcohol? Some diseases can develop silently that affect your sexual functioning. Diabetes is the most common. You may want to arrange a complete examination to rule out physical causes.

If health isn't a problem, then you and your partner need to talk about what's changed in your lives. You may not be getting what you want from your relationship. Maybe you've moved. Maybe you've added children to your life. You may be feeling isolated and angry. Use the communication exercises we discuss in "Communicating," p. 194, to help work through your problem. Work on relaxation and anxiety reduction as well.

Pain with Intercourse

An early step when intercourse is painful is examination by a gynecologist or other physician. If your pelvic area is normal, then you need to take control of your lovemaking.

Painful intercourse very often occurs because your partner is controlling the timing, position, and depth of thrusting in intercourse. The vagina lengthens and enlarges with sexual arousal to accommodate almost any size penis, but it doesn't respond instantly. You need to be properly stimulated first.

(1) You should be thoroughly lubricated. (See "Lubrication," p. 204.)

(2) Have your partner insert a lubricated finger into your vagina. You should *push out* against his finger. Pushing out opens up your vagina for easier penetration. Your partner can start with a smaller finger and work up to a larger finger. At first he should insert a finger without moving it. Then he should begin moving it, imitating the thrusting of a penis, slowly increasing depth of penetration and speed.

(3) Allow yourself to be the receiver, totally. Have your partner stimulate you manually/orally to the best and longest orgasm possible. He should stimulate you vaginally as well as orally. If possible, locate and have your partner stimulate your internal trigger area or G spot. Don't allow this important step to be rushed. See Chapter V, "ESO: Giving a Woman Pleasure," for more instructions.

(4) Now take charge. If your partner is not erect at this point, stimulate him manually/orally until he is. See Chapter VI, "ESO: Giving a Man Pleasure," for appropriate techniques.

(5) Choose a position for intercourse where you have a greater degree of control. Rear-entry, female-on-top, and side-to-side positions are usually best. *You* control the speed and extent of penetration. *You* determine the amount and type of thrusting, ranging from none at all to vigorous. Feel perfectly free to stimulate your clitoris at the same time. Remember to keep pushing out against your partner's penis.

(6) Practice this exercise until you have an orgasm with your partner's penis inserted. You need your partner's cooperation. He should realize that this problem can be solved more easily if he's helpful and nonjudgmental. The process can be as enjoyable for him as it is for you.

Problems Common to Both Sexes

Discrepancy of Desire Between Partners

The most frequent common problem is a discrepancy of desire between partners. One partner wants to make love more often than the other.

Not long ago we worked with a stockbroker and his wife, Scott and Rebecca. Scott's interest in sex had declined with a drop in the stock market and he experienced occasional loss of erection. The couple's lovemaking decreased to once a month and Rebecca missed it. We encouraged Scott to allow himself to have sexual fantasies—specifically, to recall past pleasurable sexual experiences. Fantasizing awakened his interest to the extent that he agreed to practice ESO training assignments with his wife. We assigned a schedule of days as well as of exercises and asked Scott to follow the schedule regardless of fluctuations in the Dow-Jones average or in his mood. He resisted at first, but as Rebecca got more sexual attention from him and began having several orgasms a week, he began enjoying her reaction to his attention. She, in turn, was so pleased with the improvement in their sex life that she started complimenting and encouraging him again. Scott's confidence returned. He returned to his previous level of sexual interest and to reliable, longer-lasting erections. The stock market's caprices bothered him much less than before.

Communication is crucial when there's a difference of desire between partners. Often the problem isn't sexual at all. It's a problem in some other area of the couple's lives. One partner may be angry with the other. Both people need to talk. Use the communication structures discussed in "Communicating," p. 194, to help you get started.

You may need to arrange to focus more attention on sex. You can do that by deliberately creating sexual times together, as we discussed in Chapter II, "Creating the Conditions for Pleasure."

It can help a partner with lower sexual interest if partners share erotic media—X-rated films, magazines, books, or videotapes. The materials may not be intensely arousing in themselves—that's a matter of personal preference—but they serve to focus both partners' attention on sex. Any number of people go through their lives struggling simply to handle every day's complex details. They find it difficult suddenly to switch to a mood of sexual arousal. Erotic material can help them make the transition, because it calls attention to sex without concentrating that attention on the immediate relationship—it's shared rather than confrontational.

Ideally both partners should share erotic media. It's a myth that women aren't interested. Studies show that women respond to erotic media with increased lubrication even when they report no interest. Couples who see X-rated films together are more likely to make love in the next twenty-four hours than couples who see non-X-rated films.

ESO training is an excellent way to equalize differences in desire. All it requires of you is the willingness to follow the ESO exercises that you both agree to do. After you have both thoroughly understood the content of this book by reading it through twice and discussing it, agree on which exercises you will do on which particular days. You should do the agreed-upon exercises at least three times every week, though more often is better. Your goal is not specifically orgasm. Your goal is more general: pleasurable feelings and pleasurable thoughts. Tell yourself, "This feels good; I'm enjoying myself." *It's okay if one of you enjoys the experience more than the other.*

No Partner

Men and women without partners can improve their sexual skills and the quality of their sexual experiences. These improvements will help them move to higher levels of pleasure when they select a partner who shares a desire to extend orgasmic experience. It's possible to experience Phase I ESO without a partner. But Phase II ESO requires a partner of like mind. That's because two partners fully attending one at a time multiplies each partner's sexual power.

Even without a partner you can extend your range of arousal and increase your pleasure significantly beyond your present level. You can do this by refining your self-stimulation skills. The basic information you need to do so is contained in Chapter III, "Developing Skills"; Chapter V, "ESO: Giving a Woman Pleasure"; and Chapter VI, "ESO: Giving a Man Pleasure."

A man, for example, can work toward lasting longer, setting five minutes as a goal, then ten, then fifteen, until he can maintain himself at a high level of arousal, near the point of ejaculatory inevitability, for thirty minutes. He should practice "peaking" himself—stopping just short of ejaculation—many, many times. Most men give up after about six peaks. A man should be able to peak himself at least fifteen to thirty times at a single session. He can experiment with different positions, different strokes, different locations, different lubricants, different kinds of erotic media. He can learn to increase the number of contractions with each ejaculation and the number of ejaculations during each session of pleasuring. All these activities train him for sex with a partner and, equally important, keep him sexually active. Both body and mind require sexual stimulation for optimal health and well-being. Older men especially should keep up sexual stimulation, because it's harder to recover with age when it's neglected.

Men and women both tend to use self-stimulation quickly for tension relief. A woman without a partner should also push beyond her present sexual limitations. If she's preorgasmic, she can become orgasmic. If she hasn't tried a vibrator, she may buy one and use it. If she's orgasmic but not multiorgasmic, she can learn to have several orgasms when she stimulates herself. She can usually also increase the number and strength of contractions she experiences with each orgasm. This in turn will prepare her for ESO with a partner.

An orgasm a day is a healthy, pleasurable goal for men and women of every age, with a partner or alone.

Communicating

Good communication is vital to good sex. Without open, honest discussion between you and your partner, the information in this book will be less useful to you. Changing your sexual relationship will bring up fears, hopes, anger, anxiety, resistances. It will lead to changes that extend beyond the sexual into the personal and even the social areas of your lives. You must not only practice to learn ESO: you must also talk. You must *listen* to your partner. Talk and listen objectively, without anger, fear, or condemnation.

Besides the very useful Withholds exercise we discussed on p. 64, we've included some communication exercises here. We've met people who consider such exercises silly. We've discussed that sense of self-consciousness before. You can find your way through silliness by accepting it and even enjoying its temporary relief from dignity. These exercises are games with big rewards. They're also a way of formalizing good communication. Do at least one of them every day. If you do them regularly, you'll find eventually that you've incorporated them into your routine communication. Then they won't be exercises anymore. They'll be skills you've mastered.

Agreement

The first step to take with any communication exercise is agreeing to do the exercise. That means asking your partner, "John, I'd like to do a Withhold exercise with you. Okay?" And John then has the option of saying "Yes, that's fine," or "No, this isn't really a good time. How about an hour from now, after I've finished this work?"

If a partner doesn't want to do an exercise, he should propose an alternative time. A flat *no* cuts off communication.

The Volcano

The Volcano is a general blowing off of steam. You're mad as hell and you aren't going to take it anymore. You aren't mad at your partner. Your partner's role is to listen sympathetically. You propose a time limit—one minute, two minutes, three minutes. Your partner agrees to listen for that long. Then you blow: your job, the traffic ticket you got, the tax returns due next week, the unfairness of it all. In this exercise you can give your emotions free rein. When you're finished unloading, your partner says only, "Thank you," using a neutral tone of voice and without further discussion. And because your partner listened, you feel better and you both feel closer.

The Trim

It's particularly important to deal promptly and openly with anger, which is always a component of sexual change. The Trim can serve that purpose. It's a Volcano exercise directed at your partner. You spend a minute or two or three letting your partner know how you feel about something that concerns his or her behavior.

"I'm really angry about what you've been getting away with lately. You're not paying attention to me and you never care about me and you're always critical and you're not giving the kids any time and you're not taking care of your responsibilities around the house and I hate it. What the hell is wrong with you?" Your partner then says, neutrally, "Thank you."

You agree not to hit below the belt: not to bring up subjects that you know are particularly painful, unfair, off limits, such as a previous spouse or an old relationship, a lost job, a weight problem.

Your partner agrees to listen and not to comment beyond saying "Thank you." Your partner also agrees not to discuss your criticism unless you agree to allow that discussion, and in any case not for at least thirty minutes after you've finished.

After those thirty minutes, your partner may ask you if you're willing to discuss one or more of your criticisms. You may then say yes, you're willing, or no, you're not. If you're not willing to discuss your criticism yet, you can indicate when you will be. One response, of course, is "Never." Your partner then has the option of discussing your "Never" when *your* turn comes around to be Trimmed.

The Trim isn't meant to cause gratuitous pain. You'll be cheating if you use it purely to wound. It serves two purposes: it allows you to express anger you might otherwise keep to yourself for fear of starting a major argument and it allows your partner to think about your criticism before responding, which reduces defensiveness and increases understanding.

Withholds

We discuss this exercise in detail in Chapter IV, "Getting Together." Turn back there to learn it or for review. You might notice again that it's important to do sexual Withholds regularly when you're learning ESO. You can use Withholds to deal with feelings of anger. Most people can accept anger more comfortably if it's preceded by appreciation. Note that unlike the Volcano and the Trim, Withholds are delivered by both partners, giver and receiver, in a *neutral* tone of voice.

Mind Reading

We're all constantly reading each other's minds. Why not formalize the process? You ask your partner, "Jane, I'd like to read your mind. Is that okay?" Jane says "Yes." You say "I feel as if you're angry with me. I think you don't think I've been paying enough attention to you lately." Jane says "Thank you." Then she categorizes your Mind Reading with a percentage: "You're one hundred percent right. I have been feeling that." Or "No, that's one hundred percent wrong. I don't know where in the world you got that." Or "That's about twenty percent right, but it's not a big issue. I'm not mad about it. I know you have a lot on your mind."

Mind Reading is a way of checking how your partner is feeling. It's also a way of reminding yourself how impossible it is to read someone else's mind and how impossible it is for someone else to read your mind. Reminding yourself, in other words, how important communication is.

Yes/No

This exercise is individual rather than mutual. It helps people who defer to their partners so often that they privately feel walked on.

Very simply, you make an agreement with yourself to say no to three things each day that you would ordinarily agree to with unspoken reluctance. You can say no to someone else's request; you can say no to yourself about something you "should" do.

Similarly, you make an agreement with yourself to ask for three things each day that you would like but usually wouldn't seek or accept or feel you deserve.

Some people find it hard to say no. They're afraid they'll be disliked or rejected if they do. They learn by practicing, beginning with small refusals and building as their fear of rejection fades. Some people find it hard to ask, to say yes. That limits risk, too, because if you don't ask for something, you can't be rejected. In fact, the more you ask for, the more you're likely to receive. As with saying no, start with small requests and increase their scope as your fear of rejection fades.

Learning to ask is especially useful sexually. Each time you have sex ask your partner to do something that your partner might not otherwise do and that you might not otherwise ask for. "I'd love you to massage my feet first," for example. Or "We haven't used the vibrator in a while—would you be willing to include it now?"

Getting to Know You

Communication isn't only verbal. It's also, or it should also be, physical. So we've included here several exercises that combine verbal and physical activities. You'll enjoy them. They're fun.

Sexual Exploration

This exercise allows you to familiarize yourself with your partner's genitals and the feelings they sense when you touch them in specific ways and with specific strokes. It's described in detail on p. 72.

Pleasure Turns

This exercise formalizes learning to give each other pleasure. You alternate manual stimulation with discussion. It's a logical follow-up to the previous exercise, and puts what you learned there to use.

Find a comfortable position. Decide who's first. Agree how much time to allow, at least twenty minutes each. Apply a lubricant. Begin stimulating your partner for arousal. Your partner then directs you as you go: "A little higher. A little faster. Maybe slightly more pressure. There. That's good. That's wonderful."

Explore. Enjoy. Orgasm is optional.

Afterward, talk it over. Both of you will have feelings and discoveries to discuss.

An Hour of Pleasure

Very simple: intercourse is banned; every other kind of sexual pleasuring is encouraged, including oral, manual, fantasy, and role playing. The idea is to learn to express your body's full potential for pleasure and to help your partner to that pleasure as well. The hour may include resting and talking about feelings. Orgasm shouldn't be a specific goal. If it happens, enjoy it.

Requests

Also very simple: during a period you've set aside with your partner for pleasuring, ask for one new sexual pleasure. Take turns.

Taking Charge

Each partner spends half an hour doing whatever he or she wants with the other. Decide who's in charge. If it's the man, he can stimulate the woman in any way he desires. Or direct her to stimulate him in any way he desires. When it's the woman's turn, she can stimulate the man in any way that occurs to her or direct him to stimulate her exactly as she likes.

Please note that nothing specific is expected to happen during this exercise. It's free-style. It enhances feelings of sexual self-confidence. It allows freedom to express assertive sexual feelings and to receive sexual stimulation passively. If you find yourself resisting, say to yourself, "I'm enjoying this. It's fun." Repeat the phrase each time your thoughts distract you from pleasure.

Taking Charge is a deceptively simple exercise. Used frequently, it will open up many possibilities that might otherwise be missed. It can lift couples out of sexual ruts and it allows partners to express safely some of their fantasies.

Sensory Focus

Sensory Focus is light massage with ground rules. It's an excellent exercise in learning to feel pleasure over larger areas of your body. It's a simple way to relax, to move from distraction to intimacy with your partner, to pay attention to pleasure. It's always a good way to begin lovemaking.

We include here a graduated series of Sensory Focus exercises. We often direct our clients to spend a week on each step before going on to the next. When you begin practicing Sensory Focus you might follow the same procedure. Once you have moved through step four and are comfortable with all four steps, you can choose from week to week and from pleasure session to pleasure session which step you prefer at that time. Or you may want to combine one or more steps into one. Feel free to experiment. As always, the point of the exercise is discovering more pleasure.

Step I: Silent Touching (twenty minutes minimum each partner)

(1) Woman lies nude on bed or floor on her stomach. She focuses on her sensations or listens to music with her eyes closed.

(2) Man, nude, begins by touching and massaging woman's extremities—head, hands, and feet—working his way slowly toward the center of the woman's body.

(3) Working from her shoulders down her back, man starts stroking woman's body lightly, increasing pressure as he progresses.

(4) Man then gently turns woman over and repeats the process of touching and stroking on the front of her body. He does *not* focus on breasts and genitals. He may lightly touch the breasts but totally avoids the genitals.

(5) Woman takes as much pleasure from the man's stimulation as she can. She shouldn't be doing anything but feeling as good as she can allow herself to feel.

(6) Man should be experiencing the pleasure of caressing his partner and giving her pleasure.

(7) When man is finished, he gently drapes a towel over his partner's body and allows her to lie quietly for about three minutes. Then he gives her a gentle, loving kiss and helps her up.

(8) Now reverse the procedure, the woman giving the massage and the man relaxing and receiving.

Step II: Touching with Feedback (twenty minutes minimum each partner)

Repeat the same procedure as Step I, but with the partner who is being massaged giving both verbal and nonverbal direction. Each partner in turn should say what he/she is experiencing and what he/she likes and dislikes.

Many men and women hesitate to experiment sensually because they're afraid they'll do something wrong. This exercise helps break through that resistance. Do touch the genitals, but not so rhythmically or at such length that you produce high sexual arousal. See if you can discover something that you weren't aware of before about your partner's preferences. The partner being touched may physically guide the hand of the massaging partner to show how best to stroke or touch a particular area: to the thigh, for example, saying, "Please massage me here, like this . . . that tickles a little . . . more with your palm . . . that's perfect." Or "That feels nice, but a little more [or less] pressure would feel better." Allow yourself to moan or sigh with pleasure when the stroking feels good.

Afterward, spend several minutes discussing the experience, talking about what you learned and what you felt.

Step III: Genital Arousal Without Feedback (thirty minutes minimum each partner)

Lovingly stroke and touch your partner's body from head to toe; then concentrate on stimulating the genitals for arousal. Be sure to use lubricant. Enjoy the experience *without talking*. Devote equal time to each step. No orgasms or ejaculation permitted. The positions demonstrated in illustrations 1, 3, and 11 are convenient for a man stimulating a woman. The positions in illustrations 2, 6, 7, and 10 are convenient for a woman stimulating a man.

Woman stimulating man:

(1) Concentrate on stimulating the penis. Enjoy stroking the shaft first with one hand, then with two.

(2) Direct your attention to the testicles. Stroke and fondle first one, then both. Explore the effect of gently tugging and stretching the scrotum.

(3) Explore the area behind the testicles, in front of the anus—the perineum. Stimulate and rhythmically pump the buried penile base.

(4) Locate and stimulate the external prostate spot.

(5) Experiment with the sensation of stimulating the anus. In response to loving, gentle stimulation it engorges and relaxes, opening up, or clenches shut, just like your labia and vaginal opening.

(6) Stop stimulation well short of orgasm.

Man stimulating woman:

(1) Stroke, tease, and massage the breasts and nipples. Does your partner appear to enjoy this stimulation? Do the nipples engorge and erect? Try to identify the most arousing ways to stimulate them.

(2) Use one or two hands to touch, stimulate, stroke, and tease the pubic hair and inner thighs; the major labia; the minor labia.

(3) Circle around the clitoral shaft without touching it.

(4) Gently grasp the clitoral shaft between thumb and forefinger and roll it between your fingers at a rate of about once per second.

(5) Stroke the glans clitoris with two fingers.

(6) Insert your forefinger into the vagina and slowly sweep your finger clockwise and counterclockwise, noticing areas of sensitivity and response.

(7) Stoke the anus. Notice if it becomes engorged. When the anus relaxes it is aroused and wants more stimulation. If it clenches tight it is resisting and wants less stimulation.

(8) Simultaneously stimulate two of the areas you've explored, one area with each hand: the anus and the vagina, for example, or the clitoris and the anus.

Remember, *no orgasm* is permitted during this exercise. Talk about it only after you both have completed it.

Step IV: Genital Arousal with Verbal Feedback (thirty minutes minimum each partner)

This exercise proceeds like Step III, but each partner makes at least one comment to the other while each genital area is stimulated. "I like watching your labia swell." "That feels good but I can't tell exactly what you're doing." "I'm getting bored, but keep on going—I'll get back to feeling good soon." (This step is similar in some ways to the Sexual Exploration exercise except that it doesn't necessarily involve identifying your partner's anatomy or using a rating scale.)

After you've both finished doing any one of the above Sensory Focus exercises and talking over your experiences, you may decide to have intercourse or any other sexual sharing. Make sure before you go on that you get explicit verbal agreement from your partner.

Lubrication

Lubrication is absolutely essential for ESO. Delicate tissues can't be stroked for thirty minutes or an hour without the protection and reduced friction of a good lubricant. Natural body lubrication isn't enough. Neither are lightweight water-based lubricants such as lotions, creams, and jellies. Neither are oils alone. That's why we recommend heavy-duty lubrication, either a commercial lubricant such as petrolatum or Albolene, or the inexpensive mixture of mineral oil, paraffin, and petrolatum for which we gave the recipe on p. 26.

For a pleasant variation you can add a few drops of scented oil to that lubricant. Scented oils are sold in health-food stores. Coconut, jasmine, lemon, or rose are nice. You may also want to buy a decorative plastic, wood, or ceramic container, with lid, for the lubricant. Pour the lubricant into the container while it's still liquid. It will cool to its normal semisolid consistency in half an hour. Store the container near your bed.

Some people dislike using lubricants. That's a problem. Sex is basically slippery and wet—the body deals naturally in the short term with the problem artificial lubricants solve in the longer term—and it's not ever going to be dry. If you dislike lubricants but want to extend sexual pleasure, you need to work your way through your aversion. It's actually a phobia and it can be treated by progressing through small, step-by-step changes.

Start with a lightweight lubricant such as baby oil. Rub it only on your hands. Or ask your partner to rub it only on your hands or on some neutral part of your body—your arm, your knee. When you're comfortable with that application, which may take several sessions, gradually over a period of weeks apply the lubricant closer to your genitals, until you're comfortable having it applied to your genitals themselves.

Then gradually increase the viscosity and amount of the lubricant—from baby oil to a cream, from a cream to ESO lubricant—until you're adjusted to using lubricant.

If at any time along the way you feel too uncomfortable, go back one step until a sense of comfort returns. This process of desensitization may take several weeks or more. Along the way talk to your partner about how you feel, and practice relaxation.

You can help yourself work through an aversion to lubricants by deliberately experiencing them in nonsexual settings. Apply lotion to your body after bathing, for example, and pay attention to the pleasant sensations. Give your partner back rubs with lubrication and let your partner do the same for you. You might even consider taking up finger painting for a time. It's fun and good therapy.

You may choose to let your partner take responsibility for the lubricant. If your partner applies it to your genitals for you, and you don't have to touch it, you may feel more comfortable using it in lovemaking.

Lubrication serves another useful purpose: it clearly communicates that you want to make love, that sex is going to happen and there's pleasure in store. Many men and women are deliberately tentative about approaching each other sexually. They brush shoulders or touch an arm to test the waters. If their partners don't respond, they can then pretend they weren't asking (and go away with their feelings secretly hurt). But when you take out the lubricant, you're stating very clearly what you have in mind. You can't be ignored. If no sex follows, at least you'll both have to face the question of why. Applying lubricant at the beginning of a sexual encounter is often enough to melt any resistance your partner may feel to having sex.

Adding Light

If you're uncomfortable making love with the lights on, you can work your way through the problem in a series of small steps..

First decide that you want to learn to enjoy higher levels of lighting. Then you won't be limited to making love only at night. Light will help you and your partner see what you're doing when you're giving each other ESO. And it's erotically stimulating, or can be, to see your partner's body naked in arousal. These are all good reasons for learning to accept more light.

Once you've decided, you can proceed step by step, allowing at least one week to each small change. Begin with the most light you can tolerate in the room without feeling anxious. That may be a tiny night-light. It may even be a tiny night-light covered with some translucent material, like a napkin or a towel. Begin where you can, and use the beginning light level during lovemaking until you're comfortable with it. If you feel some discomfort, practice the relaxation methods discussed in Chapter VIII, "Overcoming Resistances."

When you're comfortable with the first level of lighting

you've arranged, increase it. If you started with a night-light, add another night-light. If you started with a covered night-light, uncover it. Practice lovemaking with this increased light level until you're comfortable with it.

Then increase it again, perhaps changing to a small lamp with a fifteen- or twenty-five-watt bulb, or a red bulb, or, more romantically, candles. Continue this stepwise increase in lighting until you reach a level that you and your partner both find acceptable. Dim lighting is desirable for a romantic effect, provided you can see your partner's body. Bright lights tend to be distracting.

If at any time your anxiety returns, go back to the previous light level until you're comfortable again.

Don't feel hurried. Take time to get used to each light level before going on to the next, and change levels only gradually.

It helps to discuss your feelings with your partner, especially if you've kept the lights low because you're concerned about your body. Use the communication exercises we describe in this section to guide your discussions.

Learning to Vocalize

It's useful and freeing in lovemaking to vocalize, to let out the sounds that come to your throat when you're feeling pleasure. We'd all do that naturally if we didn't grow up having to take our pleasures in secret. Silence is a learned inhibition. It keeps you from letting go and it interferes with breathing. It's easily unlearned.

Vocalizing in lovemaking serves another purpose when it's natural and unforced, as it should be: it communicates to your partner your level of sexual arousal without requiring of you the distraction of forming and speaking words.

Practice vocalizing together in a nonsexual setting. That

might be sitting in your living room. It might be lying together in bed after watching the evening news. You may want to screen your vocalizing with sound—a stereo, a radio, the TV turned up. You can practice, alone or together, in the shower, where the acoustics are flattering and the warm water helps you relax. Decide you're going to make sounds and then make them. Take turns.

Try making the sounds you think you'd make if you were feeling the most pleasure you could possibly feel, the ultimate ecstasy. Moan, cry, laugh, scream—whatever feels freeing. Breathe in and out and as you breathe out make a sound like an animal. Rattle the back of your throat. Laugh. Sob. Swear if swearing feels good. If you think you're making too much noise, hold a pillow over your face.

You'll feel silly, stupid, embarrassed. That's normal. Enjoy the experience. Talk about it.

Keep practicing in a nonsexual context until you're both comfortable with vocalizing. Then, when you're making love, don't fake it or force it, but let it come.

Learning Oral Lovemaking

Many men and women resist oral lovemaking. They've been taught that it's dirty or wrong. Or they're afraid they'll be rejected. They're concerned about the taste of their partner's secretions. Women may be afraid that they'll gag.

Oral lovemaking is another way to pleasure. It can add to arousal and to intimacy. It's sad but true that prostitutes find eager and nearly universal interest in oral sex among their clients. That's because it's intensely pleasurable and, too often, because the men's sexual partners reject oral lovemaking at home. If you don't know how to do it, you can learn. If you're anxious about doing it, you can gradually free yourself from anxiety.

Begin by *imagining* oral lovemaking while you're making love or during self-stimulation. Imagine you are kissing and licking your partner's genitals. Imagine your partner is kissing and licking yours.

Agree with your partner that you both want to learn oral lovemaking. Agree further that while you're learning, if either of you becomes too uncomfortable, you'll return to familiar lovemaking for the rest of that period of time. Agree to take turns and to proceed in small, incremental steps.

Cunnilingus

Cunnilingus (kun-ih-*ling*-us), the man orally pleasuring the woman, can begin with both partners smelling and tasting the woman's natural lubrication when she's clean and fresh. Many women (and men) are concerned about genital odor. The best way to resolve that concern is to bathe or shower together before making love, paying special attention to washing the genitals. If odor continues to be a concern, the man can apply scented oils or scented lubricant to his partner's genitals. He can adjust to the oil by applying it first to a nongenital area of his partner's body and licking it off.

We suggest you do a Sensory Focus Step III exercise (p. 202) followed by the man briefly brushing his lips over his partner's genitals. From session to session he then slowly increases the time and the intensity of his stimulating.

He should experiment with different kinds of oral stimulation: brushing with his lips, licking, light suction. Regularly alternating tongue pressure on and around the clitoris and clitoral hood with sucking the clitoris into the mouth can be highly arousing. Men usually err in the direction of excessive force. Women generally like lighter, more regular, predictable, rhythmic stimulation. Let your partner's responses guide you.

At first, orgasm shouldn't be a goal. Later, when both partners are comfortable with oral lovemaking, it can be.

Some women find their partner's physical position during cunnilingus unmanly. They can help themselves through that resistance by deciding it's mistaken and by applying the techniques discussed in Chapter VIII, "Overcoming Resistances." The kneeling-over position (illustration number 11) or the position for mutual stimulation (illustration number 5) can help alleviate this concern.

Fellatio

Women often resist fellatio (fuh-*lay*-she-oh) because they don't like the idea of their partners ejaculating in their mouth. They may dislike the taste of semen. They may feel the penis is dirty because it's also used for urination. They may be afraid of gagging, possibly from previous experience.

Bathe or shower together to assure each other of cleanliness. Uncircumcised men should draw back their foreskins and carefully wash the area. Begin with Sensory Focus Step III (p. 202). The woman then kisses the penis without taking it into her mouth. When she's comfortable doing that, at the same or a later session, she can begin taking the erect penis into her mouth. She should position herself above the penis, her partner on his back, so she can control any thrusting. She can also place her hand around the shaft of the penis to limit its movement into her mouth. These controls help her avoid gagging.

Suction isn't necessary. Simply moving the glans penis in and out of her mouth, making sure her lips cover her teeth, is highly arousing. So is licking the glans and the shaft.

Women who fear accepting their partner's semen into their mouth and who don't trust their partner's ejaculatory control can practice fellatio with a condom over the penis. Later, when they gain confidence in themselves and their partner and learn to recognize the signs of approaching ejaculation, they can pleasure their partner without using a condom.

Some women may choose never to receive their partner's semen orally. They can still give him the pleasure of fellatio, returning to manual lovemaking or intercourse for ejaculation. An excellent alternative is for the woman to take her mouth off her partner's penis just before he begins to ejaculate but keep her warm, lubricated hand moving on the glans. Under those circumstances the man may not even know the difference. She may catch the semen in a towel or tissue, wipe it up later from the man's body, or simply not worry about it.

A woman who wants to learn to enjoy fellatio to ejaculation has to accept the taste and texture of semen in her mouth and throat without gagging. The mere thought of swallowing semen can trigger the gag reflex in some women. Others find that the taste and texture of semen has the same uncomfortable effect. A woman who wants to avoid swallowing semen can practice pressing her tongue against the back of the roof of her mouth. This arrangement closes and blocks her throat. She may then spit the semen onto a tissue or a towel.

Our experience, however, indicates that most men would prefer their partners not to spit out their semen. A woman can learn to hold both semen and penis in her mouth. Saliva begins to collect after a few seconds. It dilutes the semen, changing taste and texture to make it more acceptable and pleasurable.

Some women who accept the taste of semen still have trouble swallowing it. Another way to get used to semen—taste, texture, and swallowing—is for the man to ejaculate into the woman's hand. She can then place a small amount of ejaculate in her mouth. She should savor its texture and flavor and gradually increase the amount she tastes and swallows until she can enjoy all of it.

A woman who finds it impossible to like the taste of her partner's semen can at least disguise it with flavored oil or by preparing her mouth with a flavor she prefers—a sip of wine, a piece of chocolate, a swallow of fruit juice. Semen may taste slightly sweet or slightly bitter. It may have hardly any taste at all. Alcohol, even drunk in moderation, most frequently causes bitter semen. If bitterness is a problem, a man can experiment with changes in diet.

A woman should recognize that swallowing her partner's semen can be an intensely intimate act for both partners. It can be a significant symbolic gesture of love, and many women find it a meaningful and even a spiritual experience. It can strengthen your relationship. If this possibility appeals to you, you can both train yourselves toward it.

For more on these techniques, see "Oral Lovemaking," p. 132, and "Learning Oral Lovemaking," p. 208.

Vibrators

Vibrators come in every shape and size. There are two basic kinds, those that are battery-operated and those that plug in.

Plug-in vibrators produce a more intense vibration and don't run down. They require an electrical outlet, however, and they aren't safe to use around water. Battery-operated vibrators don't vibrate as intensely, and they run down, yet they're completely portable and they're safe to use around water. They're less expensive, but they're also usually less effective.

Very few women use vibrators by inserting them into their vaginas as substitute penises. So there's no particular advantage to a penis-shaped vibrator. We assume a man invented that design. A woman usually applies a vibrator on or near her clitoris.

The two most useful plug-in vibrators are the wand kind and the kind that looks like a small electric mixer. The mixer kit usually includes a variety of detachable rubber heads. The small knob-shaped head is designed specifically for clitoral stimulation. Another attachment that is sometimes included in vibrator kits, the twig, has a forked rubber head that can stimulate the clitoris while simultaneously stimulating the G-spot area inside the vagina. Better vibrators have two speeds. Both types of vibrator, the wand and the mixer, can be found in some large department stores. Buy them without embarrassment. They *can* be and often are used for stimulating other areas of the body besides the genitals.

We find that about half our clients prefer the wand vibrator. The other half prefer the mixer. You may want to try both kinds to see which you prefer. A third type of plug-in vibrator is the Swedish design that rides on the back of the hand, held in a place with heavy steel springs looped over the palm. The springs can catch and pull pubic hairs, so this type of vibrator isn't as popular for sex.

A man can also use a vibrator for pleasure, applying it or having his partner apply it to his penis, scrotum, external prostate spot, or anal area.

If a vibrator feels too intense, even on low speed, you can reduce the intensity by wrapping it in one or more thicknesses of towel.

Jacuzzi jets make good vibrators. So do hand-held pulsating shower heads. Some women enjoy the dental appliance made by Water-Pik, normally used for oral hygiene. Its fine, precisely adjustable pulses of water can be directed pleasantly onto the clitoral area. An inexpensive rubber spray head and hose attached to a tub faucet can provide excellent stimulation. Try removing the spray head and directing the concentrated stream onto the clitoris. Adjust pressure and water temperature carefully. Start with gentle pressure and increase it as you gain experience.

BIBLIOGRAPHY

Adams, Carl. *Secrets of Marathon Masturbation*. New York: Helios Press, 1979.

Bach, G., and Wyden, P. *The Intimate Enemy*. New York: Avon Books, 1968.

Barbach, Lonnie G. *For Yourself: The Fulfillment of Female Sexuality*. Garden City, N.Y.: Doubleday, 1976.

_____. *Women Discover Orgasm: A Therapist's Guide to a New Treatment Approach*. New York: Free Press, 1980.

Brenton, Myron. *Sex Talk*. Briarcliff Manor, N.Y.: Stein & Day, 1977.

Brylin, Brian Richard. *Orgasm—The Ultimate Experience*. New York: Dell, 1973.

Butler, Robert N., and Lewis, Myrna. *Sex After Sixty: A Guide for Men and Women in Their Later Years*. New York: Harper & Row, 1976.

Campbell, H. J. *The Pleasure Areas*. New York: Delacorte Press, 1973.

Cohen, Harvey, Rosen, Raymond, and Goldstein, Leonide. "Electroencephalographic Laterality Changes During Human Sexual Orgasm." *Archives of Sexual Behavior*, 5:3 (1976), pp. 189–99.

Comfort, Alex. *The Joy of Sex*. New York: Simon & Schuster, 1974.

———. *More Joy of Sex*. New York: Simon & Schuster, 1975.

DeMartino, Manfred F. *Human Autoerotic Practices*. New York: Human Sciences Press, 1979.

Downing, George. *Massage Book*. New York: Random House, 1972.

Fisher, Seymour. *Female Orgasm*. New York: Basic Books, 1973.

Hartman, William, and Fithian, Marilyn A. *Treatment of Sexual Dysfunction: A Bio-Psycho Social Approach*. Long Beach, Cal.: Center for Marital & Sexual Studies, 1972.

Heiman, J., LoPiccolo, L., and LoPiccolo, J. *Becoming Orgasmic: A Sexual Growth Program for Women*. Englewood Cliffs, N.J.: Prentice-Hall, 1976.

Hite, Shere. *The Hite Report*. New York: Macmillan, 1976.

Inkles, Gordon. *The New Massage*. New York: Putnam, 1980.

Inkles, Gordon, and Todris, M. *The Art of Sensual Massage*. San Francisco: Straight Arrow Books, 1972.

Kaplan, Helen S. *The New Sex Therapy: Active Treatment of Sexual Dysfunctions*. New York: Brunner/Mazel, 1974.

———. *Disorders of Sexual Desire*. New York: Brunner/Mazel, 1979.

Kassorla, Irene. *Nice Girls Do*. New York: Playboy Press, 1982.

Kegel, Arnold H., M.D. "Sexual functions of the pubococcygeus muscle." *Western Journal of Surgery, Obstetrics & Gynecology*, 60:10 (Oct. 1952), pp. 521–24.

Kinsey, Alfred C., et al. *Sexual Behavior in the Human Male*. Philadelphia: Saunders, 1948.

———. *Sexual Behavior in the Human Female*. Philadelphia: Saunders, 1953.

Kline-Graber, Georgia, and Graber, Benjamin. *Woman's Orgasm*. New York: Popular Library, 1976.

Kolodny, Robert C., et al. *Textbook of Sexual Medicine*. Boston: Little, Brown, 1979.

Kulliger, J. L. *Masturbation—The Art of Self Enjoyment*. Canoga Park, Cal.: Omega Press, 1975.

Ladas, Alice Kahn, Whipple, Beverly, and Perry, John D. *The G Spot and Other Recent Discoveries About Human Sexuality.* New York: Holt, Rinehart & Winston, 1982.

Masters, William H., and Johnson, Virginia E. *Human Sexual Response.* Boston: Little, Brown, 1966.

————. *Human Sexual Inadequacy.* New York: Bantam, 1979.

Masters, William H., et al. *The Pleasure Bond: A New Look at Sexual Commitment.* Boston: Little, Brown, 1975.

Montagu, Ashley. *Touching: The Human Significance of Skin.* Revised Second Ed. New York: Harper & Row, 1978.

Nowinski, Joseph K. *Becoming Satisfied: A Man's Guide to Sexual Fulfillment.* Englewood Cliffs, N.J.: Prentice-Hall, 1982.

Penney, Alexandra. *How to Make Love to a Man.* New York: Dell, 1982.

Pietropinto, Anthony, and Simenauer, Jacqueline. *Beyond the Male Myth.* New York: Signet, 1977.

Reich, Wilhelm. *The Function of the Orgasm.* New York: Simon & Schuster, 1974.

Richards, Brian, M.D. *The Penis.* New York: Valentine Press, 1977.

Robbins, Mina, and Jensen, Gordon. "Multiple Orgasm in Males." *Journal of Sex Research*, 14:1 (Feb. 1978), pp. 21–26.

Rosenberg, Jack. *Total Orgasm.* New York: Random House, 1976.

SAR Guide for a Better Sex Life—A Self Help Program for Personal Enrichment/Education, National Sex Forum, 1523 Franklin Street, San Francisco, CA 94109, 1975.

Thorne, Edward. *Your Erotic Fantasies.* New York: Ballantine Books, 1971.

Whelan, Stanley. *Art of Erotic Massage.* New York: Signet, 1979.

Zilbergeld, Bernie. *Male Sexuality: A Guide to Sexual Fulfillment.* New York: Bantam, 1978.

INDEX

Age
  and recovery after ejaculation, 126
  and sex, 161–162
Agreement exercise, 195
Albolene, 26, 27, 204
Alcoholic beverage
  and erection, 28, 174, 178
  and lovemaking, 28
  and sexual problems, 170, 174, 178
Alcoholism, and ESO, 160
Anatomy, sexual
  differences among men and women, 42
  early development of, 40
  of female, 31–34
  of male, 36–39
  similarities in male and female, 39–41
Androgens, 29, 180
Anger
  and ESO, 160
  exercise for, 195–196
  and lovemaking, 29
Anus, 39, 109

Anxiety
  and ESO, 160
  and resistances, 146–147
  and sexual problems, 171
Arthritis
  and ESO, 160
  and orgasm, 163
Asthma, and ESO, 160

Baby oil, 205
Bathing, and ESO, 27–28
Bladder
  infection, 35
  of man, 37
  of woman, 33
Blood pressure, and ESO, 101, 122. See also High blood pressure.
Brain waves, and ESO, 100–101, 163
Breakthrough breathing, 92–93
Breathing
  breakthrough, 92–93
  to control ejaculation, 117, 119
  and lovemaking, 92–93
  and resistances, 151
Bronchitis, and ESO, 160

The Brauers conduct frequent weekend training seminars throughout the United States on "Improving Relationships, Resolving Sexual Problems, and Enhancing Sexual Potentials." These are oriented toward education for human service professionals and their partners.

For more information on these special, highly successful programs please write to:

Brauer Stress & Pain Control
  Medical Center
ESO Study Division
Box 6050
Stanford, California 94305